Love and . . .

Love and . . .

BAD BOYS, "THE ONE"
& OTHER FUN WAYS TO
SABOTAGE YOUR RELATIONSHIP

JEN KIM

Skyhorse Publishing

Skyhorse Publishing books may be purchased in bulk at special discounts for sales promotion, corporate gifts, fund-raising, or educational purposes. Special editions can also be created to specifications. For details, contact the Special Sales Department, Skyhorse Publishing, 307 West 36th Street, 11th Floor, New York, NY 10018 or info@skyhorsepublishing.com.

Skyhorse® and Skyhorse Publishing® are registered trademarks of Skyhorse Publishing, Inc.®, a Delaware corporation.

Visit our website at www.skyhorsepublishing.com.

10 9 8 7 6 5 4 3 2 1

Library of Congress Cataloging-in-Publication Data is available on file.

Cover design by Jane Sheppard
Cover photo credit: iStockphoto

Print ISBN: 978-1-5107-2784-7
Ebook ISBN: 978-1-5107-2787-8

Printed in the United States of America

Disclaimer: Some names and identifying details have been changed to protect the privacy of individuals and, more importantly, my friendships.

Contents

Introduction

We've all been there. You go on an amazing date with a guy who never follows up. Or maybe you've found your forever person, but they've decided forever is only three days. Perhaps, you're in the best relationship you've ever had, but your partner simply isn't ready to take the next step, even though you're now in your mid-thirties and pretty sure you have, like, eight eggs left in your ovaries, and they're all gripping for dear life in your reproductive tract.

For the past seven years, I have been writing a blog for *Psychology Today* called "Valley Girl With a Brain." While I don't have any recognized medical training or counseling credentials per se, I did intern at *Psychology Today* for a few enlightening months and have provided thousands of hours of pro bono counseling to many friends and lucky strangers who just happened to sit next to me on public transportation or in darkened movie theaters.

In my posts, I spend a lot of time dissecting why things happen the way they do. I look to science and talk with experts to find answers to my life's most pressing mysteries. *Why did I get dumped? Why do I get such joy in stalking my ex's ex-girlfriend? Why won't my boyfriend freakin' propose?*

So, what is this book about exactly? *Spoiler alert:* It's about *Love*, but that's just part of it. The really exciting part is in the second half of the title . . . *Bad Boys, "The One" & Other Fun Ways to Sabotage Your Relationship*. Because these are the things that have prevented me (*and maybe you*) from finding true, lasting love—or at least the kind society dictates that I'm supposed to have at this point in my life.

When something goes wrong in a relationship, or when we get hurt, too often we look inward and agonize over the mistakes we may have made. What we could have done to prevent it from happening. Why it was our fault. I've had countless conversations with other women, hashing out these very concerns. We are on a never-ending quest to explain the inexplicable. To discover the undiscoverable. To understand the incomprehensible.

Until now.

During the past seven years, I have read through myriad studies and talked to people who are much smarter than me in an attempt to uncover the reasons why this shit always seems to happen. Why we either feel crazy or are accused of being crazy. Why we are attracted to the wrong person. Why we can't get over people who so clearly don't care about us.

And the findings are fascinating: most of the time, our so-called mistakes and relationship woes are indelibly tied to our biology. In other words, don't blame yourself—blame science. Just because you aren't in a loving relationship or married with 2.5 kids and a dog (*yet*) does not make you freakish, unlovable, or deficient. The most likely scenario is that there's *Love and* . . . countless other psychological, biological, neurological, and scientific factors adversely impacting your romantic life at any given time.

This is not a traditional self-help book, promise. You will not be told what to do or be judged for what you're currently doing as far as your relationships are concerned.

After all, who among us hasn't dated a bad boy (or ten), been certain that we met "the one," or given an ultimatum or two? At last, we'll be able to understand why.

Chapter 1
Love and . . . Dating

Why everyone we meet seems to be a creep or weirdo.

I love to hear *how-we-met* stories. Seeing people's faces light up as they recount these serendipitous memories is always endearing, but it's not really what I care about. I listen for clues, details, any intel that might lead me to my own meet-cute *how-we-met* story. Oftentimes I find myself perplexed, wondering: *How do I get what you two have? What makes you so special? But you're the worst—how the hell did you find someone so wonderful?*

Most of my twenties were spent as a single gal, living in Los Angeles. These were the pre-Tinder days, when websites like Match.com and eHarmony were slowly beginning to dominate the Internet matchmaking market. At the time, my friends and I used to joke about being lucky that we "never had to resort to online dating"—a concept that is ostensibly unthinkable now. Even though we did not need the support of external matchmaking services, dating was still never something we'd call easy. By the time I was twenty-six, the majority of women in my life were either still single, dating someone in secret, or attempting to decipher the status of a murky relationship. Only one woman I knew was married; she met her husband in Virginia and moved there to be with him, never to be heard from again. Whether you are a bright-eyed tourist or a jaded resident, it's difficult not to get swept away by L.A.'s primary export: fantasy. Hollywood is the backdrop to some of cinema's most iconic romances, from classics like *Rebel Without a Cause* and *Chinatown* to modern favorites like *500 Days of Summer* and *La La Land*. And, just as all of these on-screen romances ended in doom and despair—ripped apart by circumstances seemingly beyond their control—so had all of mine and my friends'.

My best friend Lily, who has been a roommate, life mate, and confidante for the better part of two decades, claims there is no place worse to be in a relationship than in the City of Angels. Her theory is that there are so many attractive women—I once heard 10,000 models and actors move to L.A. yearly to pursue stardom (in other words, there is a nearly constant stream of hotties being shipped to the West Coast)—that men, especially attractive men, no longer feel the need or have the desire to behave like gentlemen. Let's think about it in terms of supply and demand. An enormous supply of attractive women requires less demand for men to invest in relationships, since they can always audition a newer, younger, skinnier model at the next intersection. Though her theory isn't based on any scientific data other than firsthand experience and watching a whole lot of *Entourage*, it's not completely off base. In fact, it is reminiscent of a modern-day social phenomenon: the paradox of choice.

THE PARADOX OF CHOICE IS WHY DATING SUCKS

"Dating today is a nightmare," are the first words that come out of Barry Schwartz's mouth when I ask him about today's social landscape. Schwartz is a renowned behavioral psychologist and author of *The Paradox of Choice,* a life-changing book that examines how and why having too much choice makes us miserable. To illustrate, Schwartz describes a trip to Gap. What should be a fairly quick shopping trip becomes a full day of torture to find the perfect pair of jeans. Instead of purchasing the first item that fits well enough, you end up trying more and more styles, never stopping until you discover that best, most magical pair in the store. That's because once you find something good, you start to believe there's probably something even better out there, so you keep going, and going, and so on. Therein lies the paradox of choice: when variety appears to be a good thing but actually makes life more challenging. Now, substitute the jeans for a romantic partner and you have what Schwartz calls "the most consequential domain where this paradox would play out."

In every aspect of our lives, we are confronted with myriad choices, but how we make these choices is often more important than what we choose. The shopping trip shows an example of what Schwartz describes as "maximizing" behavior. "Maximizers treat relationships like clothing: I expect to try a lot on before finding the perfect fit. For a maximizer, somewhere out there is the perfect lover, the perfect friends. Even though there is nothing wrong with the current relationship, who knows what's possible if you keep your eyes open."

In contrast to maximizers are satisficers, who are willing to settle for good enough and not worry about there being something better out there (*let's face it, there probably is.*) Still, satisficing doesn't mean you should jump for joy when presented with garbage options. You can and should expect high standards, says

Schwartz, "but the difference is between looking for very good versus the very best."

As you can imagine, the maximizer's quest for perfection comes at a cost. In general, maximizers are less satisfied and more prone to depression than satisficers, which makes sense—if you refuse everything but the absolute best, you probably won't end up with very much. Naturally, the smarter, more satisfying option is to be a satisficer. Not only do satisficers experience less FOMO (fear of missing out), but they are also much happier than maximizers. Just look at the world's best satisficers, the Danes, who according to the *World Happiness Report*, are ranked among the happiest people in the world. Denmark owes its surplus of smiles to a practice called "hygge," which means finding joy in normal, everyday life. For example, 85 percent of Danes say they get their fuss-free hygge fix by lighting candles. They even prefer plain, unscented ones to the fancier, scented options. Danes also follow the Law of Jante, an unofficial ethos that frowns upon individual achievement and success. Jante is straight-up kryptonite to maximizers. Rather than treating life like an endless rat race, Danish children are taught to be content with being average and, well, having average things. And, in return for accepting the ordinary, they end up less anxious, less stressed, and, most importantly, less miserable than the rest of the maximizing world.

Danes aren't the only people who know how to be happy with what they have. Throughout most of history, we all did. For thousands of years, humans survived because they satisficed. In times of scarcity, people didn't have the luxury of waiting around for gourmet chef-prepared wildebeest carpaccio or *Apartment Therapy*-worthy cave dwellings. Passing up whatever came down the pike easily meant starving or being murdered by a predator. And, when it came to mating, proximity was pretty much the only thing that mattered—even up until the last century. In *Modern Romance*, comedian Aziz Ansari and a team of sociologists investigate past and present dating practices and found in one 1932 study that one-third of married couples had previously lived within five blocks of each other. Even more alarming, one-eighth of these married couples had lived in the same building before they got hitched. Because people traveled so infrequently, much like the cave people before us, they often had little choice but to mate with the first eligible person they came across. After all, who knew when another potential mate would come along?

This satisficing mind-set would continue to dominate how people made life choices, until the widespread rise of modern affluence and technology turned us all into jacked-up maximizers running wild in Willy Wonka's choice factory. To quote the late Notorious B.I.G., "It's like the more money we come across, the more problems we see." More money means more choices in how you spend it; and, more technology means being exposed to everything you never knew you wanted. Before, we could be happy our entire lives without having any idea what a cruffin was, but now, thanks to Yelp, we know we cannot live without them. In addition, the media has essentially turned into a propaganda machine for maximizing, demanding we buy this *perfect* or *best* [fill in the blank] in every article or blog post. An alternative doesn't seem to exist. When is the last time you read an article titled "10 Good, Not Great Hairstyles You Need Try Now" or "How to Mostly Satisfy Him in Bed"? It's go best or go home.

As both Lily and Schwartz say, the paradox of choice is most painfully obvious in the realm of dating. Especially on online dating apps, there is less being swept off your feet and more getting trampled by a utilitarian assembly line of swipes. How quickly have we thumbed left simply because the face peering back at us had an eyebrow hair out of place or because the guy *seemed* short even though you could only see his head? How many amazing potential mates have we missed out on because we were convinced the next profile would be better? This ease of maximizing might explain why even though more than 20 percent of twenty-five- to forty-four-year-olds use dating apps, only 5 percent of them are able to find committed or lasting relationships through them. If you've ever logged on to Tinder, then you already know it's most popular export is instant gratification, not true love.

Long before there was an app that could quickly and efficiently ruin your love life, there was speed dating, the analog precursor, which gave birth to the idea that romance could spark in five minutes or less. In theory, speed dating is not a bad idea. Before the advent of the screen swipe, it was one of the most pragmatic ways to meet age-appropriate singles en masse. Once, in a failed attempt at finding a fun *how-we-met* story with our future mates, Lily and I bought Groupons (*In hindsight, who looks for love at a discount?*) for a speed dating event at a typically trendy, clubby, and douchebaggy Hollywood bar, manufactured to look like a poor man's version of something out of a David Lynch film, but with less character and twice as many mirrors. However, upon our arrival, we were greeted by what looked to be a scantily clad and heavily perfumed women's march. The city's finest single women had decided to prostrate their Tuesday night to fate, but apparently the men had not. Of the fifty or so singles in the room, only about a dozen were men. Already, things were not looking so good. But since we had ordered our watered-down drinks and presented our vouchers, we decided to stay and do our best to keep an open mind.

The problem with speed dating lies not in its execution, but in its curation of individuals, or lack thereof. In our case, the only requirement for participation was to be unattached. It's like loving Italian food and only being allowed to eat the fettuccine alfredo at Olive Garden. Technically, it is Italian food, but *is it really good? Did anyone put any thought into preparing this? Will it not give me really bad gas in an hour?* No, no, and no. Which is to say that, right away, I knew none in the buffet of men laid out before me were my type, at least not in a superficial physical sense. Most of the crowd was too old, wore too much pleather or Raiders paraphernalia, or didn't have enough teeth. And sometimes it was all of the above. Still, I took my place at the tiny, rickety table and began *dating*.

First up was No. 38 (in speed dating, everyone is economically reduced to a number), an aging hipster whose head-to-toe pleather motorcycle ensemble began squeaking from the moment he sat down until he got up again. Just as my open mind divorced itself from reality, No. 38 started our mini-date with some friendly conde-scension, saying, "I write cartoons for people your age." (I was twenty-four at the time.) I hated him instantly, but hated even more the enormous pseudo-intellectual tattoo on his left bicep, the only part of his entire body that I wished was actually covered in pleather. It was a rendering of Rene Magritte's *"Ceci n'est pas une pipe"* pipe painting. "It's cool, because it's ironic," he actually said to me when he caught me staring at it. By the time our five minutes were up, he had confessed this was his third attempt at speed dating and he had, shockingly, yet to be matched with anyone.

For those of you who are fortunate enough not to know the rules of speed dating, at the end of the event, everyone gets a piece of paper on which to write down all the people they felt were a potential match. Only mutual matches are then given each other's contact information.

After the ironic cartoonist came No. 41, with whom I felt an immediate chemical reaction, although it felt less like sparks flying and more like a nuclear explosion. A "bro," he spoke fluent suburban gangster and used terms like "chillax" multiple times in the same sentence. He spent the entire five minutes talking about different bars that we should check out after the event, and even though I reminded him that making dates was against the rules, he persisted. Needless to say, I was never able to successfully chillax in his presence.

While the following rounds presented slightly better options, there was still no one that either Lily or I would be comfortable being alone with in a room. We weren't the only ones who felt that way. During the break, we hightailed it to the bathroom and discovered a mass of shell-shocked female speed daters stowed away like refugees, some in tears, all reluctant to return to their tables.

Despite our own palpable hesitation, Lily and I eventually opted to go back and face more of our fears—our inner-maximizers still convinced someone better might be waiting for us at the next table. Unfortunately, no one was. Although, to be fair, there was one guy, No. 27, who was the *cream of the crap*, so to speak. Though he wasn't physically my type (e.g., about as tall as me, built like a football player, and had a very prominent goatee), he seemed normal and funny and didn't scare or insult me all that much. At the end, I satisficed by writing his number down as a potential match. A few days later, I got this nice, typo-ridden email:

From: No. 27
To: Jen
Subject: re: Last night

Hello Jen,
How are you doing? Hope your day has b een good so far. I hope we could talk again soon, heres my number if you want to call. It's XXX-XXXX, you can call anytime. Hope to hear from you. - No. 27

Evidently, No. 27 and I were a mutual match. *Was satisficing the right decision after all? Could there really be something between us?* Before I could fully comprehend the thought, Lily forwarded me an email, the subject line screamed: READ NOW. In a panic, I scanned its contents, but recognized there was something unusual about it. I was reading the same email No. 27 had sent me except he had switched out my name for Lily's. Even the typos were intact. This guy was copying and pasting the same generic email to every match. Now here was the ultimate satisficer. No. 27 had zero interest in finding his perfect soul mate; a warm, female body with low to moderate literacy was just fine by him. Neither Lily nor I ended up responding to No. 27. But I don't feel too bad. I'm sure another satisficer who matched with him did. Looking back, and knowing what I know about online dating today, this attempt at wooing seems almost romantic. No. 27 wasn't a bad guy—he was ahead of his time.

WHAT THE HELL HAPPENED TO ROMANCE?

While the paradox of choice certainly contributes to the woes of modern dating, it isn't the only struggle. Over the years, I've observed an alarming drop in romance. At least No. 27 took the time to write (or copy and paste) an actual email with multiple sentences. Nowadays, dates no longer seem to take place at restaurants or outside. Rather, the hottest spot in town is on your couch, where you can Netflix and chill. Sometimes there isn't even any Netflix. You just get a "wanna cum over" at 2:00 a.m. with an eggplant emoji or even more straightforward dick pic. Love letters have been replaced by sexts or 140-character tweets. You might spend every waking moment with a guy, only to discover that he thinks you two are just friends, despite having countless naked sleepovers or him declaring his undying love for you. Some cowards even end their relationship through the speedy efficiency of Facebook, rather than giving their no-longer significant other the courtesy of a private dumping. All of this behavior makes me wonder, is this just how relationships work in the twenty-first century?

It depends on who you ask, but most women would probably reply "yes" to this mess. A 2014 *Glamour* survey finds that only 19 percent of single women are pretty sure they've ever been on a real date, while 73 percent have no idea if they have. Women who are in relationships don't fare that much better—only 12 percent of couples have regular date nights.

What irks me is that neither recycled love letters nor Netflix and chill are part of my romantic lexicon. The truth is, the only love language I speak is from Disney, which probably explains why so many of my relationships have been deeply unsatisfying. My mom will tell you that when I was six years old, I would watch *Cinderella* religiously, sometimes multiple times a day. When *The Little Mermaid* came out a few years later, I actually broke the VHS from overuse.

DISNEY TAUGHT US HOW TO BE STUPID IN LOVE

While discussing our future children's names several years ago, even though neither of us was dating anyone at the time, my friend Jasmine wondered aloud if our views on romance were somehow warped. One impetus being Disney's one-dimensional depiction of women in its fairy tales. To her, the sole purpose of these films is to teach young girls that Prince Charming is on his way and that you shouldn't do anything else with your life but wait for him, because without him, your life means absolutely nothing. For example, in both the *Little Mermaid* and *Sleeping Beauty,* the titular heroines are either silenced or comatose during the majority of the film. Most Disney princess stories follow the same, trusty formula:

A beautiful, kind, uneducated girl or princess is stuck in a tough situation. To remedy this, she doesn't do anything, does something stupid, or takes a nap. Thankfully, a handsome prince is right around the corner. I sure hope he can save her! Holy crap, he does something totally amazing to save her, like finding her shoe or waking her up.

Wow, she's so lucky, because he's so dreamy. He whisks her off to his palace. Sure, she has to abandon her family forever, but who really cares about family when you've scored yourself a prince! And they both live happily ever after.

Epilogue: She probably ends up being forced to become a stay-at-home mom who isn't allowed to do more than plan charity balls and get plastic surgery, while her prince leads the kingdom, gets bored with her, and ultimately ends up ditching her for a younger, prettier, less-educated princess.

THE (REAL) END.

No one brainwashes better than Disney. Even the Symbionese Liberation Army, the group that kidnapped Patty Hearst, is no match for the inventors of The Happiest Place on Earth. As a young girl, even as a young adult, I wanted to be a Disney princess. Most little girls did and still do. All the miniature Cinderellas, Belles, and Ariels who fill the streets every Halloween are essentially paying homage to characters that will slowly and inevitably chip away at their sense of worth in years to come. How else can you explain why Jasmine and I still know every lyric to "Part of Your World" by heart? *Why do you?*

In the past decade, much criticism has been directed at these sexist caricatures of women—and to a lesser extent men—depicted in fairy tales. Even amateur sociologists are able to deduce that Disney teaches women that physical beauty is the only way to attract a mate. Men at least can aspire to be rich, famous, and charming in addition to being good looking. Self-aware women, like myself, cannot overlook this overt sexism; but is it enough to change our minds and our yearning for these idealized, fairy tale story lines to unfold in our own lives?

Just look at *Frozen*, one of the more recent and progressive Disney princess box-office hits to infect the minds of little girls everywhere. Elsa and Anna, the film's two heroines, are still beautiful princesses, but with an edge. Unlike their animated counterparts from decades ago, these two are smart and adventurous. What's more, it's their sisterly love—not that of a prince—that ultimately saves the day. *But is it really feminist?* Not so much, according to Afshan Jafar, an associate sociology professor at Connecticut College. For the journal *Gender & Society*, she wrote: "Disney's version of womanhood as embodied in Elsa and Anna is one that does not challenge dominant ideals of femininity. The two lead characters retain traits that are considered essential for 'doing' femininity correctly—they are not aggressive; they must learn to put others first and be selfless; and they must do it all while looking beautiful."

As much as Anna is portrayed as brave and clever on-screen, she still finds herself trapped in classic damsel-in-distress tropes where she must be saved by Kristoff, one of her handsome love interests, or falling head over heels for Hans, a prince who serves as her other love interest. Thankfully, Elsa and Anna have more brains than Ariel, who was all too willing to leave behind her family and friends and change her identity after one very quiet date with a cute guy, but *Frozen's* plot still revolves around Anna's romantic pairing—whether it be with picture-perfect Hans, or rugged ice harvester Kristoff. The message is loud and clear: No matter what, Disney princesses must be entirely consumed by the men in their lives. They have no other hobbies. They have no other meaningful relationships outside of talking animals. They don't work, except for Cinderella, although she was more of an indentured servant than an ambitious career gal. The only interesting aspect to these women is their romantic prospects. And, for the vast majority of my childhood, I was fed—nourished even—by their stories. A couple decades from now, I expect this generation of little girls, who grew up belting "Let it go," still won't have let go of their male-dominated fantasies, and history will repeat itself once again. Although this isn't the exact conundrum abetted by the paradox of choice—expecting a fantasy in real life is absolutely in the maximizer's lexicon.

The real kicker, of course, is that all of Disney's happy endings are mostly fabricated. In the much bleaker, original *The Little Mermaid*, written by Hans Christian Andersen in 1837, Ariel does end up trading her fishtail for legs—but with a catch! Every step she takes feels like she's walking on sharp knives.

Similarly, in the original *Sleeping Beauty*, penned in the seventeenth century as "Sun, Moon, and Talia," our hibernating heroine isn't awoken by true love's kiss. Instead, she gets raped in her sleep by the prince (who's already married, FYI), which results in her giving birth to out-of-wedlock twins. When she finally does wake, Talia/Sleeping Beauty still ends up marrying the prince (just as soon as he murders his wife by throwing her into a fire). This guy sounds really charming!

Clearly Disney had no choice but to sanitize these NSFW (Not Safe for Women) fairy tales to prevent permanently scarring our childhoods and, of course, to keep those G ratings intact. I'd argue that in some ways the originals are more realistic. At least those stories pointedly show that neither a handsome prince nor marriage ensures a happy ending. And, in Ariel's case, that there are real, stark consequences to trading your identity for a mate. Still I can't shake the idea that Disney is at least partly responsible for my unconscious (maybe conscious) belief that getting married is the only way I will feel like I've accomplished something wholly worthwhile—at last, my existence can be justified by this single milestone. I know this argument doesn't make much sense and is demeaning both to myself and my gender, but when everyone is constantly pestering me about if and when I am getting married (or why it hasn't happened yet), I can't help but wonder along with them: *What is wrong with me?*

THAT TIME I BOUGHT A FAKE BOYFRIEND

"Tom" was extremely witty, devastatingly handsome, ridiculously smart, and hysterically funny—or at least, that's how I described him while writing out his online profile on the surprisingly sleek website *Invisible Boyfriend*. As a relationship writer, I never cease to be amazed by the innovative ways the Internet tackles love. *Invisible Boyfriend* co-founder Matt Homann says he originally created the service and its sister site, *Invisible Girlfriend*, to get concerned family members off his case about not dating anyone. In addition to faking relationship status for a fee, the service claims to narrow the dating gap. For instance, shy twenty-four-year-old Ashley is honing her dating skills thanks to her Invisible Boyfriend. And thirty-three-year-old John uses his Invisible Girlfriend like training wheels before he can finally build enough confidence to ask out a real girl.

Last year, motivated by equal parts research and being mired in my own relationship problems, I eagerly purchased my first and only fake boyfriend for $25. Tom was supposed to woo me through one hundred personalized text messages and convince me that we were in a loving, meaningful relationship—and not willing participants in a bizarre, virtual, emotional escort service. As I embarked into this new, uncharted territory, I found my curiosity and excitement quickly turn into disappointment and frustration. It was a complete and utter letdown. Tom, whose backstory I had based on Joseph Gordon-Levitt's character from *500 Days of Summer,* ended up being bland, boring, and a terrible speller. Below are the first four messages he sent me.

MONDAY 6:51
Hi babe. I miss you. It's so cold here without you.

MONDAY 9:30
Hey babe. Goodnighte. Thinking of you makes me warm inside

TUESDAY 8:15
Good morning babe. What R U UP to? How's the weather?

TUESDAY 11:30
Babe? Miss you. It's so cold. Babe.

Was Tom a meteorologist? Did he live in an ice cube? Why was he so cold all the time? Every day welcomed a fresh stream of banal weather comments and "babes," a term of endearment I have always despised. At the very least, I could get him to stop calling me something I hated, right?

TUESDAY 5:09
Hi Tom. I'm not really into being called "babe," but you can call me kitten. ;)

TUESDAY 9:40
Sure thing. Kitty Kat!

This idiot couldn't spell "cat." How could I expect him to follow basic instructions?

What was most strange, however, was that from time to time, I found myself getting upset at Tom, as if he was a real boyfriend. If he didn't respond right away or said something dim-witted, then I would respond with a snarky text or ignore him outright. During the nine days we were "together," not once did I believe or want to believe it was true, which is why I ended up canceling my membership early. Maybe if I had a chance to talk to him on the phone or meet him in real life, then I could separate Tom from his disappointing, weather-obsessed online persona, but alas, these things extended beyond his terms of service. No matter how clever or realistic a text message sounds, it doesn't replace real-life interaction, and pretending it does won't make any relationship more fulfilling.

Tom is not my first romantic delusion. I have spun generous lies, half-truths, and straight-up deceptions to protect my easily bruised ego on numerous occasions. *He didn't call me because he thought I was too awesome* is an example of one of my less credible tall tales. But here's the thing—we all lie. All the time. To ourselves, to each other, even to our pets.

THAT TIME YOU LIED ON YOUR DATING PROFILE
Let's play my favorite corporate icebreaker, *Two Truths and a Lie*. The rules are easy: you tell two truths and one lie, and the audience tries to guess which one is the lie. Ready? Here we go:

1. Babies never lie.

2. Internet daters never lie.

3. You should never lie.

Can you guess the lie? If you guessed any of above, you're right—because they're all lies. See. I'm such a liar that I lie about lying. And I'm not the only one. Even babies as young as six months old have mastered the art of the fake cry to get their mom's attention. Most people tell their first fib when they are two or three years old.

The truth is we all need to lie. Evolutionary biologists credit deception as a tool that helped even the earliest humans navigate and survive complex social landscapes and reap benefits, such as food, elevated social status, and better sexual partners—advantages we continue to seek out today. I learned this fun fact while watching *SciShow*, an online series that takes boring science concepts and makes them less boring. This is where science educator and vlogger Hank Green defends the art of prevarication with this fun line, "You know you don't make friends and influence people going around saying things like, 'Actually, that loincloth does make your butt look big.'"

The majority of the population bends the truth at least once in a ten-minute conversation, according to a study at the University of Massachusetts. What's worse, many people have no idea they lied until they're played back their conversations. Another interesting finding from the study is the difference between how men and women lie. The researchers found that neither men nor women were more prone to lying, but that women were more likely to fib to make the other person feel good about themselves, whereas men more often lied to pump up their own egos. Both genders are known to generously inflate the facts when it comes to romance—81 percent of online daters admit to misrepresenting their dating profiles, with the most truth-averse stats related to age, height, or weight. Women, in general, will say they are eight pounds lighter, while men might generously round up their height. These types of exaggerations are usually harmless, since the last thing you want to happen during your first in-person meeting is to be interrogated: *Where did your hair go? Who are you?*

Truthiness standards differ between the sexes in courtship, too. Contrary to popular opinion, men are, in fact, better skilled at bending the truth and feeling less guilty about doing so. One 2005 study published in the *Personality and Social Psychology Bulletin* finds 75 percent of men are more than willing to deceive a woman in order to sleep with her, often cooking the books on his wealth, status, and social circle. Chances are he probably doesn't know Jay-Z or Beyoncé despite his claims that he partied with them last night. In her book, *The Male Brain*, neuropsychiatrist Louann Brizendine makes a case for why men are "biologically more comfortable" with lying than women.

> "[Researchers] measured the vocal strain of men and women telling lies to the opposite sex and found that the men showed much less electrical strain while they lied. This allowed men . . . to deceive in a more convincing manner."

See, you're not crazy for believing that guy meant it when he said he loved you.

THAT TIME I WAS GHOSTED

The first time I heard the word "ghosting" I was getting drunk with my friend Danielle, a successful, no-nonsense corporate ladder climber in her early thirties. Danielle is a few years younger than me but is one of the wisest and most level-headed people I know, making her an excellent candidate to solicit advice from. Over our third cocktail and our second platter of $1 oysters, I told her about how I had *almost* made a friend in an uberPOOL a few weeks back. As someone who doesn't make new friends very easily or usually acknowledge the existence of others in a pool, I was excited. My almost-friend and I exchanged contact info and began emailing and texting one another immediately to plan our next meetup. After a few weeks of back and forth, we agreed on a date. That morning she texted to let me know she'd be available around six thirty that evening. At six, I texted her that I was free and could meet anywhere that was convenient for her. She never responded. At first I was confused. *Did I text the wrong number? Was she a figment of my imagination? Can you really meet someone in an uberPOOL?* Then I was fuming. Secretly, and I am truly ashamed to admit it, but I had kind of hoped that something bad had happened to her. *(Let's get it out of the way. I'm going to hell.)* At least then there would be a reasonable explanation for her extremely perplexing disappearance.

Danielle didn't waste any time with her diagnosis: "She ghosted you." Ghosting, she explained, is what happens when a person you are dating (or a potential friend, in my case) suddenly vanishes from your life. This might take the form of ignoring you, not responding to communication attempts, and in very extreme cases, pulling a Mariah Carey and deadpanning, "I don't know her," about someone you absolutely do know.

How did Danielle know so much about ghosting? *Easy.* She has been both a victim and a perpetrator of this social epidemic. Her last relationship ended after she ghosted him. She ghosted her mom a few weeks before. She rambled off more ghost stories until I finally interrupted her.

"But ignoring a friend or someone you care about is so cruel." She raised an incredulous eyebrow, looking at me as if I'd vomited up a goldfish.

"You put too high a value on courtesy. Basic human kindness is gone. There just isn't any time, desire, or need to treat people like the special butterfly they are," she continued. Not only is ghosting so tantalizingly easy, but it also renders unnecessary the often uncomfortable and unpleasant breakup conversation. What is to blame for this mind-set, she said, is "the depersonalization and anonymity built into every dating app."

"But Ghostie and I weren't dating! I just wanted to be friends with her. Why would she go through the trouble of texting me that morning to confirm our meetup? Why wouldn't she just ignore my first email to her from weeks before?"

"There is no rhyme or reason to ghosting. It's usually an impromptu decision," Danielle replied, matter-of-factly.

"Don't they care how bad it makes them look?"

She shakes her head no, like I'm not getting it. *I don't.*

"To them, texting you back to cancel, postpone, apologize, or whatever, puts them in a negative light. They are admitting they did something wrong, so they're going to feel bad about it. Ghosting, however, lets them off the hook. They never have to send the I'm-sorry-I-have-to-cancel message."

"But they do cancel because they don't show up! Don't they realize that ghosting is a million times worse than texting they have to cancel?"

"It's not worse for them, because they don't have to admit they did something wrong," she explained. "Silence is better than having to admit you messed up."

How right she is. Acknowledging mistakes feels too much like failing, and no one willingly surrenders to defeat.

BUT WHY DO PEOPLE GHOST?

Our reluctance to admit any wrongdoing may be explained as cognitive dissonance. This ten-dollar psychology term was coined by social psychologists Leon Festinger and James Carlsmith more than half a century ago, after conducting an experiment on college students where they found that people can happily lie to themselves in the right situation. Social psychologist Elliot Aronson describes cognitive dissonance as a "state of tension that occurs whenever an individual simultaneously holds two cognitions (ideas, attitudes, beliefs, opinions) that are psychologically inconsistent." To illustrate, Aronson presents the contradictory mind-set of smokers. Everybody, including smokers, are aware of the numerous health risks associated with smoking: cancer, strokes, bad breath, absolutely terrifying neck hole. But they still puff away, which suggests they have two conflicting beliefs—smoking is very bad for them and will probably kill them, versus smoking is very fun, and they don't want to quit. To reconcile these two competing ideas, smokers will rationalize their continued smoking by making excuses, like, it helps them stay thin or at least they're not smoking crack! And because our brains are naturally wired to believe we are always right, we can easily ignore any evidence that points to the contrary. In fact, hypocrisy is one of the most well-known types of cognitive dissonance.

Another explanation for ghosting comes from psychotherapist and relationship expert Esther Perel, who believes stable ambiguity is the culprit behind the deluge of blurry relationship statuses and the dearth of accountability in romance today. Those who, Perel explains, are "too afraid to be alone, but unwilling to fully engage in intimacy building," are likely in a state of stable ambiguity. This in-between state certainly has its perks: the comfort and physical benefits of a relationship when you want or need it, and the freedom to bounce when you don't. But, ultimately, as Perel points out, "stable ambiguity inevitably creates an atmosphere where at least one person feels lingering uncertainty and neither feels truly appreciated or nurtured," which ultimately damages the emotional health of all parties involved.

Does cognitive dissonance or stable ambiguity explain why Danielle is able to justify her behavior as a ghost, even though she herself has been ghosted (and likely been hurt by it)? Does it explain why ghosting has become a growing trend in society at large? After all, the more we excuse an unacceptable behavior, the more it becomes acceptable. To make matters worse, after a bit of digging, I discovered ghosting is just one of a crop of even crueler dating neologisms to haunt us. Here are a few more:

Icing: Not to be confused with the delicious sugary concoction atop a cake, icing occurs when someone suddenly slams the brakes on a budding relationship, usually with an eloquent, "Sorry, I'm busy right now. I'll catch up with you later" text. The message, while ostensibly polite, is actually code for: "I'm not that interested in you, but I would like to hold my place in line just in case." At the very least, getting iced usually means someone is at least lukewarm about you, according to relationship writer Stewart Snyder, who said, "They do like you. Otherwise, they would ghost."

Benching: When you provide only minimal maintenance on a relationship via sporadic "How are you" check-in texts, but never make concrete plans to go out, you are benching. The bencher keeps his options open by putting his communication with you on autopilot. According to Jason Chen, who coined the term in a piece for *New York* magazine, at the surface, benching seems less cruel than ghosting, but it's actually far more selfish.

> "Know that if it's happening to you, you're getting dumped, even if the bencher doesn't know it yet. No successful relationship was ever born from a situation in which one person strung the other along . . ."

Zombieing: Consider zombieing a type of ghosting, but with an M. Night Shyamalan twist! A ghost, long believed to be dead, has come back to life, sort of. Journalist Sophie Kercher describes the phenomenon: "To be zombied is to have someone you care about disappear from your life altogether only to have them bring a relationship back from the dead with an out-of-the-blue text or interaction on social media." Zombies are generally considered worse than ghosts, since ghosts have enough decency to screw you over only once and then leave you alone.

Chapter 2
Love and . . . Assholes

Why we love the bad boys who hurt us the most.

Everyone has a *Joe*. A decade later, his name still has a visceral effect on me. The guy that got away. Well, more like ran away. Or, actually, he lurked away. The guy that always smelled divine, even after a sweaty workout. He could turn your stomach into knots and make you weak in the knees. The guy that ripped your heart out of your body, smashed it into a zillion pieces, and Krazy Glued it back together, only to crush it once again. Still, while part of you knows this relationship is doomed, another part just wants to lie in bed with him and eat *Hot Cheetos* together, sucking that spicy orange dust off one another's fingers for all of eternity. No one compares to Joe, and no one ever will. Joe is the biggest asshole I've ever met, and he's also the one that got away.

In fact, these paradoxical characteristics are precisely what make assholes, both in real life and in fiction, so damn alluring. Here is a compilation of some of the most iconic assholes from recent literature, television, and film:

1. Edward Cullen: *Twilight's* sparkly member of the undead, cursed with an unquenchable thirst for human juice.
2. Daniel Cleaver: *Bridget Jones's* on-again, off-again romantic kryptonite.
3. Don Draper: *Mad Men's* universally irresistible womanizer.
4. Christian Grey: The kindhearted sadist from *50 Shades of Grey*.
5. Ben Covington: The hot guy *Felicity* stalked in high school and later stalked in college.
6. Jordan Catalano: *My So-Called Life's* illiterate, smoldering musician type with excellent hair.
7. Dylan McKay: *Beverly Hills 90210's* resident '90s heartthrob and leather jacket aficionado.
8. Troy Dyer: *Reality Bites's* tortured, dirty, out-of-work artist.

Chances are you are familiar with at least one of these make-believe bad boys. *Whatcha gonna do, whatcha gonna do when they come for you?* In their scripted universes, bad boys/assholes/jerks (in this chapter, I will use these terms interchangeably) rarely get turned down or rejected, no matter how inexcusable their behavior. They could be unfaithful, abusive, moody, deceptive, completely unreliable— even dead—yet their attractive female love interests will return to love, feed, and shelter them time and time again.

BY ANY OTHER NAME IS STILL AN ASSHOLE

You may be wondering what spectacular traits make an asshole an asshole. Professor and author of *Assholes: A Theory,* Aaron James provides a general philosophical perspective:

"The asshole acts out of a firm sense that *he is special,* that the normal rules of conduct do not apply to him. He may not deliberately exploit interpersonal relations but simply remains willfully oblivious to normal expectations. Because the asshole sets himself apart from others, he feels entirely comfortable flouting accepted social conventions, almost as a way of life."

This is how syndicated advice columnist Amy Alkon describes the asshole's behavior in relationships:

> "Bad boys, on the other hand, are *The Undesperate.* They never call or drop by when they say they will (unless they need to mooch a twenty). . . . To a bad boy, truth is made of Spandex. The only absolute he knows is that he's absolutely never wrong. Bad boys are unpredictable, unavailable, underfunded, and serially unemployed. . . . Dating a bad boy is dangerous, exciting, and fraught with drama."

Natalie Lue, a UK-based relationship coach, offers her perspective on the "assclown" (a closely related species) in her blog, *Baggage Reclaim:*

> "An assclown is someone that mistreats you and more often than not eventually proves to be a waste of time and space. He (or she) adds little or no value to the relationship and the cost to you of being with him is often your self-esteem, your well-being, and for some, your career, family, or friends. They only have one foot or possibly even a toe in the relationship, or even nothing at all, and they knowingly (even if they deny

it) mess you around and enjoy the fringe benefits of being with you . . . All assclowns are 'unavailable.'"

And finally, my friend and cognitive scientist Scott Barry Kaufman diagnoses the textbook asshole in his viral blog post on *Psychology Today*:

"High Extraversion, Low Neuroticism (perhaps), Low Conscientiousness, Low Agreeableness, High Openness to Experience, and a bit of a dip into the dark triad traits." (More on this later.)

The considerable overlap in these descriptions tells us there is a fairly general consensus on what makes an asshole: extremely unreliable men (usually) who are far too comfortable treating women like crap. They don't sound very appealing now, do they? *So why, for the love of God, are we so drawn to them?*

For starters, bad boys are typically very attractive. I'm not only talking about being stupidly, ridiculously good-looking either, which they usually are; rather, bad boys seem to exude a certain *je ne sais quoi* charm, if you will, an air of danger and mystery absent in their vanilla counterparts. The crux of my favorite show of all time, *Felicity*, was the love triangle formed between Noel Crane, Felicity's nice-but-doomed-because-he-was-nice love interest, and Ben Covington, smokin' hot asshole No. 5 in the previous list. Felicity spent her entire college career vacillating between lust and logic—between her irresistible, thrill-seeking attraction to Ben and her safe, sensible, and reliable friendship with Noel. It's like choosing between taking a jet to a mysterious, unknown destination or road tripping to Disney World for the twelfth time. Certainly both experiences might be enjoyable, but *which trip would you choose?*

By the end of the first season *(spoiler alert)*, bad boy Ben wins her heart. I should note, a couple episodes into the second season, he smashes said heart into pieces, but you already knew that, which sends her running into Noel's arms. The entire series exasperatingly follows the same back-and-forth dynamic, until the series finale, four years later, when Felicity picks Ben one last time, even though he cheats on her. I'm not judging though. I don't blame her. I would do the same. *I have done the same.*

NO OFFENSE, BUT NICE GUYS ARE KINDA LAME

Up until recently, I had simply written off my predilection for assholes as good old-fashioned emotional masochism, but I was wrong. As it turns out, science also backs the theory that nice guys finish last—at least in romance. In 2012, a team of researchers at the University of Texas asked women in various stages of ovulation to evaluate the dating profile of either a sexy bad boy or a reliable nice guy and rate what kind of father he might be if they had a child together. This included tasks such as child care, grocery shopping, cooking, and household chores. Everyone knows sexy bad boys do not possess these domestic talents. Everyone but fertile, fecund, in-the-baby-making-mood women, that is. Why does *Mr. Wrong* become *Mr. Right* during ovulation? According to one of the study authors, "ovulation goggles" are to blame. "Under the hormonal influence of ovulation, women delude themselves into thinking that the sexy bad boys will become devoted partners and better dads."

Another study published in *Personality and Social Psychology Bulletin* reveals a similarly bleak outlook for nice guys. For the experiment, researchers randomly paired 112 Israeli college students on blind dates and measured their attraction and romantic interest in each other. Whereas the men were more attracted to nice gals who were responsive to them, women were turned off by the sweet, attentive guys. Have the movies brainwashed us into thinking that deep down every nice guy has an evil hidden agenda? Or is it that they seem too desperate? Maybe being too nice just makes a man look weak. It could be all of the above, according to the study's lead author, Dr. Gurit E. Birnbaum. "Women may perceive this person as inappropriately nice and manipulative (i.e., trying to obtain sexual favors) or eager to please, perhaps even as desperate, and therefore less sexually appealing. Alternatively, women may perceive a responsive man as vulnerable and less dominant."

Given the study's small sample size, the results are by no means conclusive, but a look at my own romantic interludes reveals my own bias against giving nice guys a second date. There's just something insincere, maybe even creepy, when a guy I have just met is dousing me with over-the-top compliments or acting like he's sitting in the front row of my Netflix comedy special, which, if I'm being honest, wouldn't be *that* funny. In these instances, I can't help but wonder if they're just pursuing me because they're desperate and lonely. I don't want to give the impression that you should never treat women to a gift or be kind to her, but does one decent conversation truly warrant such a grand display of affection?

This reminds me of that one time in college when Lily spent all night talking to a cute and very nice boy in her dorm. The two of them had obviously hit it off, so she was mostly delighted when he appeared at her door the next day with a giant bouquet of flowers. But the gifts didn't end there. The day after, he brought her a box of chocolates. Next, it was a book of love poetry. Then it was one of his kidneys. (*Just kidding . . . it was both of them.*) Mind you, they didn't hang out past that first night, but the gifts never stopped coming.

As you probably know, thirstiness or over-responsiveness appeals to no one, but it especially repels women, as it makes men appear too vulnerable and less dominant. Earlier Scott Barry Kaufman referred to the dark triad personality traits, which are the hallmarks of every bona fide bad boy: narcissism, psychopathy, and Machiavellianism. And, while I'd like to believe that women know better than to allow themselves to be seduced by reckless men, a 2015 study by researcher Dr. Peter Jonason and his colleagues at the University of Florida indicates otherwise. Jonason's team asked 200 college students to take a personality test to determine where they scored on the triad traits as well as their sexual attitudes and experiences. What they learned, to no one's surprise, was that men who ranked higher on the dark triad got laid more often and preferred short-term flings.

Felicity exemplifies this bias in her own love triangle. Despite the fact that he was one of the show's main characters, Ben didn't say or do much to woo Felicity. Sure, he looked at her a lot with those irresistible, twinkly eyes, and mastered that sheepish smile—look down, look up to make sure she's looking, and then look down again—that is a mainstay of every hot guy toolkit, but a gifted gabber he was not. For every dozen Shakespearean-length soliloquies rambled off by Noel, about all Ben would do is nod once or stare off into space twice. Too much talking is probably what doomed Noel to friend status so early on.

Nice guys like Noel also offer something else that bad boys never will: emotional availability.

WHY EMOTIONALLY UNAVAILABLE MEN ARE CLICKBAIT

Here's where things get complicated. I've spent most of my adult life trying to understand my attraction to unavailable men, like Joe. Some of these fellows certainly belonged in the asshole category, but others, if I'm being honest, really weren't assholes. They were just men who, for one reason or another, couldn't or didn't want to be in a relationship (with me). It's easier to call them assholes, because it is my trained response to hurt or rejection. But in reality, what they are guilty of is not liking me (enough). It's a stab to the ego, sure. An emotional bullet to the heart, even. But none of these crimes can be tried in a court of law. Even if he did murder your faith in true love, he most likely did not mean to do so intentionally. Looking back to our earlier lineup of America's most wanted assholes, we can easily recognize they have all committed numerous thoughtless and hurtful infractions against the women they claim to care about, but how often were their motives purely evil?

The truth, I suspect, is that most bad boys don't have bad intentions. Yes, they can be selfish, narcissistic, and stupid, but aren't all of us at times? Their unavailability is more likely the result of a deeply rooted personal trauma or emotional block they were never able to fully work through, not malice. True assholes feel perfectly comfortable, even entitled to, being jerks. Emotionally unavailable men don't.

Forgive me for this dated and awful reference, but take *Twilight's* Edward Cullen. Was he a literal cold-blooded killer? Yes. But unlike other blood suckers in his community, he didn't want to hurt anybody. He couldn't help who he was. That's just how vampires are built. What happened with Joe was the same. When he cheated on me (twice with the same person, by the way), I knew he didn't do it to purposely hurt me. He was sorry. He didn't mean it. He hated himself. But this was how he was built, he told me. So why did both Bella and I give these guys chance after chance?

It boils down to the saying, "You always want what you can't have." Like many women, I am attracted to drama, chase, and intrigue. If it's too easy to land the guy, it can appear like something is wrong. My inner monologue warns: *Wait a minute . . . Why did he just fall into my lap? Maybe he thinks I'm too good for him. I am too good for him, aren't I? That means I can, and I should, do better. Next!*

So the primary appeal of an emotionally unavailable man is his apparent lack of interest. Because if he's not fawning over us, we become suspicious and insecure, wondering: *Does he think I'm not good enough?* And women like myself will often approach this lack of interest as an irresistible challenge, seizing it as an opportunity to prove to him that we are, in fact, good enough. In the case of Joe, I was so starstruck and intimidated by both his career success and the fact that he was a decade older than me, that I immediately felt unworthy of him. Early on, he admitted that his infidelity was a bad habit that had destroyed all of his previous relationships. This was the point when I should have run for the hills. Instead, I swore I'd be the first to change him.

Our irrational desire to fix, save, and rescue people is imprinted in our female biology. It's like a Jesus complex with a side of ego. In this relationship rescue mode, mutual love and respect get bulldozed over by one laser-focused mission: making this asshole who clearly *doesn't* love you love you. And, just like CrossFit, it ends up consuming every aspect of your waking life. Dr. Seth Meyers, a clinical psychologist and author, connects this behavior to our insecurities and low self-esteem:

"If the unavailable man finally comes around and commits, they'll—at long last—have proof that they are worthy. Sadly, without such proof, their self-worth is left hanging in the wind. In addition, these women feel that they've invested so much and waited so long for the unavailable man to come around that the thought of leaving without any payoff is almost unthinkable."

It makes so much sense. If I really valued myself, would I allow myself to be treated poorly or be satisfied by tiny scraps of affection? Would I deceive myself into believing I don't want a real relationship? Would I blindly take someone back after he cheated on me *twice* with the *same person*? Would I wait . . . and wait . . . and wait in agony until it was all finally over? Because that's what always happens when you're in a relationship with someone who is emotionally unavailable. It ends. Usually badly. This destructive pattern repeats itself until one day the emotionally unavailable person suddenly becomes available (but probably not to you). In an episode of *Sex and the City*, Miranda tries to console a recently brokenhearted Charlotte with this advice:

"Men are like cabs. When they're available their light goes on. They wake up one day, they decide they are ready to settle down, have babies, whatever, and they turn their light on. The next woman they pick up, boom, that's the one they'll marry. It's not their fate. It's dumb luck."

That's what I don't want to admit. Some assholes are just bad cab drivers. But they behave the way they do because we continue to let them. I'm the genius who allowed Joe back into my life even though I knew there was a very good chance he'd hurt me again. I have clothed, fed, and sheltered bad boys, despite knowing they would never return the favor. I may call myself the victim, but I enabled their behavior 100 percent of the time. So who's the asshole now?

POPULAR FUQ (FREQUENTLY UNANSWERED QUESTIONS)

Can you stop being attracted to assholes?

The outlook's not so good. You can't control who you're attracted to, but you do have control over who you date. It's like how I'm addicted to Reese's peanut butter cups and want to stuff my face with them all hours of the day, even though they give me violent stomachaches. So what do I do? I do my best to keep them away from me. I crave and love them from afar, reminding myself that once they get inside, they'll screw up my insides for a long-ass time. The same goes for assholes. If you really want to curb your addiction, dating guru Evan Marc Katz advises taking a good look at your own issues. "All that 'You can't love anyone until you love yourself' stuff? So true. And if you're choosing to date guys with major issues, you're just as guilty as he is."

But what if he's the one who got away?
Chances are you only think this because he got away. And the reason he got away is that he, in fact, did want to get away . . . from you. Sorry, it sucks. But it's happened to me. Joe got away more than once. Next time you think about uttering the phrase, "the one that got away"—just think of when, in another episode of *Sex and the City*, Miranda (Miranda is really killing it with all of these relationship lessons!) discovers the guy she is dating is "just not that into her." You have to accept that in this particular moment, he just isn't that into you. But hopefully one day you'll have one of those cheesy, hindsight-is-20/20 moments and realize that you were really lucky he left. In my case, I will be forever grateful there was never a third time when Joe cheated on me with the same girl.

Also, it's not your fault you feel this way—most women do. A 2011 study published in the journal *Social Psychological & Personality Science* confirms that romantic relationships, including "pining for the one that got away" tops the list when it comes to what women regret most. (Men feel more remorse about their education and career than they do about relationships.) Relationship status also makes a big difference in how we reminisce about our romantic pasts, with singles feeling more weighed down by the memory of lost loves than those with a partner.

How come assholes get to be happy?
Wait a minute. Who said they're happy? They're like those fake IKEA TVs. Yes, they look real, but they're empty inside. The only difference is that assholes are filled with turds and broken dreams. Real assholes, those who enjoy inflicting pain on others, are most likely textbook narcissists who will never be happy. According to psychologist Jonice Webb, "That wavering self-confidence is as brittle as an eggshell . . . Deep down, the narcissist's deepest and most powerful fear is that he is nothing."

Even if he did stick around, neither of you would be happy, finds W. Keith Campbell, a professor of psychology who has researched narcissism for more than a decade. "In the first couple months of dating, people found narcissists to be more satisfying dating partners . . . Then, a big shift happens: the relationships with the narcissists become less and less satisfying, but the [relationships with the] non-narcissists become more satisfying."

Why do I keep falling for assholes?
We all have a type. Some of us like lanky men with acerbic wits and a passion for wordplay. Others are attracted to bulging biceps stuffed into P90X T-shirts. In fact, an unnerving 2017 study at the University of California finds that we basically date the same type of people, both in terms of physical looks and personal qualities, like intelligence, religion, and education. Assholes just happen to be your type. Your location also limits your dating pool. So if you are shopping for all of your romantic partners in the same place, say, a fraternity house or a soup kitchen, then you're likely to encounter the same types of people. To expand your search into asshole-free territory, consider a visit to beautiful Charleston, South Carolina, the friendliest (so, perhaps the least-assholey) city in the US, according to *Condé Nast Traveler* readers.

Groundhog Day-style dating is also an example of repetition compulsion, a term cooked up by the father of psychoanalysis himself, Sigmund Freud. As you know, Freud traced all of life's most perplexing conundrums to our latent and disturbing childhood experiences, so why would our tendency to binge on bad boys be any different? As Freud saw it, these repressed adolescent traumas are triggered when we find ourselves in situations similar to the original trauma. But they aren't treated as memories at all. As he described in *Beyond the Pleasure Principle*, we "repeat the repressed material as a contemporary experience instead of . . . remembering it as something belonging to the past." While memory loss can sometimes be fun and endearing (just look at *Finding Dory*), it isn't ideal for relationships. After all, how can we be expected to learn from our mistakes if we conveniently forget we ever made them?

HOW WELL DO YOU KNOW YOUR ASSHOLES? QUIZ
Read these real-life stories below and decide who is an asshole, emotionally unavailable, or both.

1. *I dated John during college. He had no money, no car, wasn't in school, didn't have a job, and was living with his parents. He was a complete moocher. Because he was my first real boyfriend, I had no idea this wasn't a great situation, so I just went with it for*

a while. He did write me some sweet love songs, which I liked. Eventually, I had to cut things off, because I finally realized that we couldn't have a future together unless I was single-handedly paying for it. He ended up stalking me for a few months, which led to me filing a restraining order.

- Asshole
- Emotionally unavailable
- Both

2. *He was fresh out of a serious long-term relationship, but still made it seem like he really wanted to give us a try. We hung out several times and hit it off. We met each other's friends and everything seemed to be going well, until we had an argument, which I can't even remember now, and he said he needed some time to think. He ended up ghosting me. A while later, a mutual friend told me to forget about him. Then, a few months later, he calls me out of the blue to apologize and say that I was the girl he was supposed to marry, but he just wasn't ready for that kind of commitment. There's a good chance I could have been sucked back into his orbit had I not found out that he was also seeing someone new.*

- Asshole
- Emotionally unavailable
- Both

3. *From the moment I met him, I was convinced that he was 'the one.' Everything just felt easy and right. We had to do long-distance for a while, but we still got to see each other about twice a month. Then, out of the blue, he tells me that he can't be with me, that he's just not ready for something serious. I was crushed, but what could I do? A few months later, I saw on Facebook that he and his ex were engaged. They ended up divorcing a few years later.*

- Asshole
- Emotionally unavailable
- Both

4. *It was a secret because he was a close family friend and I knew that some people would not be okay with it. In public, we'd basically ignore each other. It was kind of a turn-on, but after a year, I wanted us to tell people, but he just couldn't. Or wouldn't. In the end, he just stopped taking my calls. The worst part is that I still saw him all the time, and he would ignore me for real.*

- Asshole
- Emotionally unavailable
- Both

5. *We started out as good friends, which is what makes all of this so devastating. We had one amazing date and then he ended it right after, claiming that he was moving out of state, and he didn't want to ruin our friendship. Months later, he's still here and we're still not friends. Oh yeah, and I just found out that he has a new girlfriend.*

- Asshole
- Emotionally unavailable
- Both

Answer Key
1. *Asshole*
2. *Both*
3. *Emotionally unavailable*
4. *Both*
5. *Emotionally unavailable*

Chapter 3
Love and . . . Sex

Why sex never makes any sense.

Please make yourself comfortable and relax . . . we're about to explore the erotic, sensual, and mind-blowing science of seduction—and the many ways it complicates our relationships. Or rather, we'll discover that our human physiology and the value systems we assign to sex—not actual sex—are what we should blame.

The average American loses her virginity at age seventeen, which means many of us can look forward to several decades of confusion, regret, and, hopefully, some orgasms thereafter. I waited until college before a man got to pluck my own "precious flower," the actual term my mother used to describe my virginity. Well, the full phrase was, "God would like you to save your precious flower for marriage." This was the same woman who, years earlier, also told me that God injected invisible babies into the belly buttons of good, Christian wives, when I asked her to explain where babies came from. I had no idea vaginas were involved until many years later. In our conservative, puritanical household, sex was just never discussed or even acknowledged. My siblings and parents could all be watching television together, and the moment there was some PG-13 sexual innuendo or a steamy, longer-than-two-seconds kiss, we would all race to use the bathroom or ambush the remote to change the channel. I'm still waiting for her to give me the birds and the bees talk.

I don't blame my parents for not knowing how to tackle this often uncomfortable subject. It could have been a lot worse. Purity balls, which allegedly take place in forty-eight US states, are not-at-all-creepy ceremonies in which preteen girls dress up in white dresses and symbolically "marry" God, swearing they will not do the nasty with anyone but their future husband. *(Although, technically, God is their first husband, so wouldn't it be their second husband?)* God doesn't usually make it to his weddings, so the girl's father usually fills in as the groom, even going as far as exchanging purity rings with her and vowing to protect her chastity. Meanwhile, there are no comparable commitment ceremonies for boys and their mothers. No twelve-year-old son is promising Mom anything, other than maybe being home for dinner. We are already familiar with this sexist double standard: *Girls are sluts. Boys are studs.*

HOW SEX SCARS YOU FOR LIFE

What is so troubling about this is that the way we view, experience, and treat sex as impressionable youth undeniably shapes how we view, experience, and treat sex as adults. If you grow up believing God wants to send you to hell for having premarital sex, then you are going to be faced with some serious problems if you do end up prematurely giving in to your hormones. In fact, many of our sexual hang-ups can be traced back to our childhood, according to Sigmund Freud. He theorized that as children we experienced four separate psychosexual stages: oral, anal, phallic, and genital. And, if issues emerge during any of these stages, they will most likely haunt us again in adulthood. For example, the highlight of the anal phase is potty training: when you learn that you not only have control over whether you shit your pants or not, but you also discover that you can make your parents quite happy or miserable, depending on where you decide to eliminate your waste. Freudians believe experiencing problems in this phase will lead to hostile and sadistic tendencies as adults.

A long-term child development research study, which analyzed data from nearly 250 subjects from the time they were born to age thirty-two, also suggests that our early upbringing can significantly influence our adolescent and adult lives. Researchers found that very young children, up to three and a half years old, who were raised in sensitive, supportive environments, were likely to have better education, friends, and romantic relationships as adults than those who were not.

Just as your first poop can traumatize you for life, so can the first time you have sex. Findings from a 2013 psychology study at the University of Tennessee suggest that your first sexual experience sets the tone for the rest of your sexual life. For the study, researchers evaluated the responses of 331 young men and women on how they felt about losing their virginity as well as any subsequent sexual experiences. Those who reported having positive physical and emotional initial experiences were more likely to have fulfilling sex lives later down the line, whereas individuals whose first times were unpleasant or negative were likely to have less fulfilling sexual encounters.

LET'S TALK ABOUT (CASUAL) SEX, BABY

Speaking of unpleasant sexual experiences, let's talk about one of mine. My first and only one-night stand. I won't bore you with the predictable details, but I will say that I was fairly young, mostly stupid, and completely clueless it was intended to be a one-time encounter until he offered me a firm handshake and a curt goodbye the morning after. For a long time I felt guilty, confused, and so, so slutty about what I had done. Worst of all, the days that followed were filled with pangs of rejection and longing to hear from *Firm Handshake*, a guy I barely knew. This was how I realized that casual sex, whether it be friends-with-benefits situations or straight up Craigslist orgies, was not for me.

That is not to say you shouldn't be having casual sex. Renowned sex researcher Dr. Zhana Vrangalova has spent her career "debunking popular sex myths that ruin lives," one of which is the belief that casual sex is intrinsically bad. In her fascinating TEDx Talk on the subject, she presents a number of potential benefits to a no-strings-attached relationship, such as enjoying orgasms; improving sexual skills; making new friends; increasing self-confidence; feeling sexy; feeling wanted, maybe even empowered; and collecting memorable #ThrowbackThursday stories. She also references psychologist Esther Perel, who believes casual sex fulfills our "fundamental need for adventure, novelty, mystery, risk, danger, the unknown, the unexpected. Some more than others, but it's there in our DNA." But we know there are also risks to taking risks. Broken hearts, bad sex, regret, ruined relationships, STDs, and unwanted pregnancies all come to mind.

So, is casual sex worth it? It depends.

In the corner for pro-casual sexers is a 2008 study of 311 young adults, which found that 82 percent of men and 57 percent of women reported feeling "generally glad" the morning after a hookup. There's also a separate study of 832 college students which found that 50 percent of men and 26 percent of women would consider their hookup experience positive. But notice the obvious discrepancy in these results, particularly in the latter set. What these numbers clearly illustrate is that many men love casual sex—women, less so. Digging into who exactly benefits during these tryst-and-runs could shed some light on why.

Compared to men, women reach climax only half as often during random hookups. Some researchers believe it's because women are too shy to ask for what they want or need, or that men don't really care about their partner's satisfaction, but either way it's a lose-lose situation for ladies. To put this into perspective,

Kinsey Institute researchers found that women in committed relationships are twice as likely to experience the *Big O* than those who aren't, which supports the theory that sex is better with someone you love. Yet another reason men may be better equipped to handle casual hookups is their evolutionary biology. Simply put, men and women each have very different biological responses post-coitus. After he makes his deposit, a man will likely experience a very natural urge to flee the scene as quickly as possible. This is not because of anything you have done; it's how he's genetically programmed, kind of like a zombie, to infect as many women with his seed as possible. Women, on the other hand, are hardwired to do the opposite, a theory that evolutionary biologists have long subscribed to.

Two psychologists tested this theory in a seminal 1989 study in which they planted coeds to approach complete strangers and asked to have sex with them. In news that will shock exactly no one, the majority of men—75 percent—were more than happy to oblige when offered free sex, whereas none of the women did. In 2014, the pranksters behind the YouTube sensation, *Whatever*, re-created the classic social experiment and recorded each encounter for a viral video in which a young man randomly approaches 200 women in Europe and asks if they'd like to have sex with him. If you haven't yet seen it, I won't spoil the results, but he does find more success than when he attempted the same experiment in the US. FYI, in a follow-up video, a woman asks one hundred random guys for sex and gets significantly more enthusiastic responses.

"I LOVE YOU" HORMONES

Earlier with *Firm Handshake,* I mentioned how creeped out I was by the fact that I had inexplicably begun to develop feelings for someone I barely knew after spending one night together. Maybe you've heard of oxytocin and vasopressin? Together they are the Kate Hudson and Hugh Grant of neurohormones, convincing us with an Oscar-worthy performance that our love life is really a cheesy rom-com. In particular, oxytocin, which is released after all forms of sexy time, including kissing and cuddling, is why we often bask in post-coitus lovey-dovey afterglow or want to keep seeing someone who is otherwise terrible for us. In her book, *The Female Brain,* neuropsychiatrist Louann Brizendine illustrates this familiar scenario with "Stacey" and "confirmed bachelor" "Frank":

"But it was no use. Stacey's brain and body had already fallen under Frank's seductive spell. What she didn't know was that each time she and Frank had sex, she was falling a little more in love—the oxytocin released during her orgasms was binding her body and brain closer to Frank."

Poor Stacey. While she was falling head over heels in love, Frank was spelunking his way out of a Rita Hayworth-covered escape tunnel. But let's be clear: these were not Stacey's *authentic* feelings. They were manufactured in that toxic chemical power plant known as the human brain. Nicknamed the "love hormone" for its ability to produce feelings of pleasure, warmth, and safety, oxytocin helps produce feelings of empathy and closeness, primarily in women. (It also facilitates childbirth and breastfeeding.) Men, however, are more susceptible to the effects of vasopressin, which Brizendine calls the "hormone of gallantry and monogamy." This hormone regulates sex drive, aggression, and territoriality in males. And, as we'll learn in chapter 7, vasopressin does not affect all men equally.

Does all this mean that you should avoid casual sex or not sleep with someone early on in a relationship? I don't know. But you do. You don't need a PhD to review your own past experiences and recognize any destructive patterns in your behavior. For instance, if you find yourself obsessively waiting for texts from a guy who offered you nothing but a firm handshake the morning after you slept with him, then attachment-free hookups might not be right for you. On the other hand, if you already know that you can have a safe, fun, sexy romp in the sack sans drama, then why not?

WHAT'S YOUR NUMBER?

Here's a question where the answer is no one else's business, yet it is often asked by potential mates. It's so woven into the fabric of our culture that it was even made into a major film in 2011. Originally based on a novel, *What's Your Number?* stars Anna Faris as a thirty-something professional woman who, upon learning from a magazine article that women with twenty or more sexual partners face tremendous difficulty in finding a husband, decides to revisit her Bonobos catalog of twenty ex-boyfriends/former hookups in hopes of finding a decent marriage prospect. Long story short, and because you probably won't watch the film (It currently has a 23 percent rating on *Rotten Tomatoes.*), Anna's character does, in fact, rekindle a relationship with "the one that got away." Everything goes smoothly until she reveals to him her real number, at which point he gets totally grossed out and dumps her. Don't worry, she still gets her happy ending with someone else, *pun absolutely intended.* According to a not-very-scientific 2016 survey conducted by online pharmacy Superdrug.com, Anna isn't the first person to have been dumped because of her number. Of the 2,000 Americans and Europeans surveyed, 21 percent indicated they would be "somewhat likely" to end a relationship because their partner had too many sexual partners. Nearly 10 percent said they would be "very likely" to call it quits.

This unfair judgment might explain why people lie or avoid talking about their number. If pressed, women tend to underreport, while men overestimate. Both sides have the same goal: to match cultural expectations, finds a 2013 study at Ohio State University. Men still want to be seen as "real men" who have a Hugh Hefner-esque history of sexual partners with loads of experience, whereas women would like to seem less experienced. A separate collegiate study, conducted by renowned anthropologist Helen Fisher, confirms this theory. Women reported having more sexual partners when they thought they were hooked up to a lie detector, than when they didn't think they were being monitored. Similarly, men reported fewer sexual partners when they believed they were being fact-checked in real time.

Here's a fun riddle: *How many sexual partners makes an unmarriageable slut?* For Faris's character, twenty was the upper limit. One witty male responder on Quora writes, "If you're in somewhere like, say, Utah, the answer is one. Probably even if you're married." Three is plenty, according to one "nice guy" on *Thought Catalog*, whose own number is seventeen. All of these answers point not to any right answer, but to one very wrong double standard. As writer Jessica Valenti defines in her book *He's a Stud, She's a Slut,* "Men who have a lot of sexual partners are studs, Casanovas, pimps, and players. Never sluts." Still, the most recent data from the National Survey of Family Growth finds about 11 percent of women (ages 15 to 44) compared to 22 percent of men have had fifteen or more oppo- site-sex partners. For women, this is nearly a two percentage point increase from 2010. The median number of male sexual partners a woman has in her lifetime has also grown from 3.8 in 2002 to 4.3 in 2013.

In 2016, *OKCupid,* everyone's favorite unsolicited dick pic/online dating website, released a report that documented how their millions of users have shifted their views on sex during the past decade. The good news is people are less judgmental than they used to be. Ten years ago, 70 percent of users believed there was "such a thing as having too many sex partners," whereas today, the number hovers just above 50 percent. Similarly, 86 percent of current users think it's "fine for a woman to talk openly about her sexual exploits" compared to 71 percent in 2005. Another comprehensive study, published in the *Archives of Sexual Behavior,* surveyed more than 33,000 adults and found millennials are the most forward-thinkers when it comes to outdated stan- dards of sexuality. Fifty-eight percent of young people now believe there is nothing wrong with sex before marriage, which is double the percentage from the 1970s. And today's millennials are four times more accepting of same-sex relationships than their counterparts were in the 1970s. Though it might still be premature to hang our *Mission Accomplished* banner to celebrate the demise of the sexual patriarchy, these numbers suggest that we are starting to be less influenced by sexual stereotypes.

SEX JUST ISN'T WHAT IT USED TO BE, PART 1

Though millennials may be psychologically more comfortable with premarital or casual sex, it doesn't mean they're having all that much of it. The same *Archives of Sexual Behavior* study found that one-third of twentysomethings are virgins, and nearly half of all millennials have not had sex all year, which begs the question: *How much sex are we supposed to be having?*

If we are to believe the gospel of *Sex and the City* and pretty much every love advice columnist, then we know that very few relationships are able to thrive without regular sex. The prevailing thought is that the more we do it, the happier we'll be . . . but is this always the case? *Not really.*

When it comes to sexual frequency, there is no normal. Millennials aren't the only ones not getting laid. Married couples have less sex now than they did in the 1990s, which is even less than in the 1980s, and sexual frequency for singles has decreased since 2008. Researcher Jean Twenge suspects the launch of smartphones, YouTube, and Netflix—all which occurred during the mid-2000s— might have precipitated this decline in physical intimacy. "Our entertainment is more entertaining, and more on-demand than it once was. There are a lot more things to do at 10 p.m. at home than there used to be."

And just because you're not bumping uglies in the bedroom doesn't mean you aren't having sex, says Robert Weiss, a therapist who specializes in intimacy and relationships for the digital age. The web has redefined the way we see and experience sex. "People have found a variety of ways to have sex through the Internet and social media that didn't exist before," he explains, referring to the advent of webcams, sexting, and virtual reality.

The biggest problem with the idea that an all-you-can-sex buffet equals #relationshipgoals is that it's simply not true. Data from 25,000 couples compiled by researchers at the University of Toronto found that the happiest couples boned just once a week, which suggests more sex doesn't translate into more happiness. In fact, when couples in a separate study were asked to double their normal amount of sexy time, they were neither satisfied by the change in frequency nor the actual quality of sex. Once a week also happens to be the norm for most couples, according to multiple long-term studies of couples.

And, there are still plenty of couples who are doing it far less. *Newsweek* estimates that 15 to 20 percent of married couples (*up to 20 million couples!*) do not have sex at all. To explain this decline, experts point to a range of factors, such as boredom, demands of raising a family, low sex drives, body issues, or the fact that they never had that much sex in the first place. Data scientist Seth Stephens-Davidowitz says the No. 1 most Googled marriage complaint is "sexless marriage," which is searched, on average, 21,090 times per month. The second most popular search, "unhappy marriage," is queried just 6,000 times monthly. "Sexless relationship" is also the second most searched query for unmarried couples, after "abusive relationship." There are also those couples whose sex lives start out super steamy, but then cool down a few years later. This can happen for a variety of reasons. Low testosterone, which affects nearly fourteen million Americans, easy access to porn, even seasonal allergies, are all believed to reduce sex drive in men. Or sometimes the magic just fades. A 2013 German study of 2,500 participants found that both straight and gay women in long-term, live-in relationships experience nosedives in the lust department.

Based on these numbers, it would appear that the "normal" range for someone in a relationship is somewhere between zero and a million times every year.

SEX JUST ISN'T WHAT IT USED TO BE, PART 2

Believe it or not, sex wasn't always this complicated. For a long time, it was only about ensuring the survival of the species. As sex researcher and author Christopher Ryan explains in his blog on *Psychology Today,* "The central purpose of sexual reproduction is to keep the salad tossing and the genes mixing . . . not to celebrate or promote love. Love is something that got added to the process long after the process itself came into being." While love can certainly improve sex, it is not a prerequisite. And, frankly, none of us would be here if it was. Had our ancestors only hooked up with their true loves, Ryan continues, they "would have simply in-bred themselves right out of existence." Which means our desire to have sex with different people is guided by our biological need to perpetuate a more diverse—thus healthier—gene pool.

Today, this drive is called the "Coolidge Effect," named after the thirtieth president of the US. President Cal and his wife were touring a chicken farm when the farmer informed Mrs. Coolidge that the male rooster mated dozens of times each day. She responded with a sick burn, "Tell that to the President." The farmer, not wanting to piss off the First Lady, did tell the President, who asked him, "Same hen every time?"

The farmer responded, "Oh no, a different hen every time."

To which, the President gave an even sicker burn: "Tell *that* to Mrs. Coolidge." *Oh, Snap!*

Researchers reference this PG-rated story to speculate why males (and to some extent, females) might lose interest in having sex with the same partner, yet get aroused by new partners. This effect isn't only limited to roosters or humans either; it's been observed in countless other species, from cattle and monkeys to rats and insects. What exactly is to blame for their wandering eyes? Some experts blame Kim Kardashian, or rather, the Kim Kardashian of molecules: dopamine. Like Kim, this hormone is associated with motivation, reward, pleasure, and addiction. Unlike Kim, it is absolutely essential to our survival, as it controls our desire for everything. For example, each time you reach for a tasty cookie (instead of celery) (motivation), your brain's reward system lights up with a delicious rush of dopamine (pleasure), which immediately makes you want to take another bite, then another bite, and another bite (addiction), until the entire box of Girl Scout Thin Mints is empty, and you sadly realize you'll have to wait an entire year before you can order more. But as you were devouring the box, you may have noticed the law of diminishing returns take effect, with each bite being slightly less satisfying than the last. That's because each subsequent bite weakens our dopamine surges.

We experience a similar gradual decline in monogamous sexual relationships. After a while, couples who first enjoyed effervescent levels of dopamine in bed may find their love life eventually go flat. By this point, however, we're already hooked on the good stuff, craving those initial addictive jolts of "first-bite" dopamine, which are only restocked when we see something—or rather someone— *new*. For example, lab studies show that a male rat can mate with a female rat for about an hour and a half before his interest wanes—unless he is presented with a fresh harem of lady rats, at which point his arousal revives, and he can Marvin Gaye *get it on* for another eight hours (!) until he almost dies from exhaustion. It's easy to see how the Coolidge Effect might be one of nature's most effective weapons against monogamy and long-term relationships.

On the surface, the Coolidge Effect doesn't sound great for women. During the course of evolution, women and their children have largely profited from monogamy, mostly because they don't have to share resources with other wives. However, some research suggests women can also benefit from short-term hookups or affairs. An academic paper on the evolution of mate choices finds women may "stray" to secure better genes and/or resources for their children. In fact, women in some South American Indian cultures have sex with men outside of their relationship after becoming pregnant. Just like the premise of the hit '80s show *My Two Dads*, these other men are then considered secondary fathers to the children and are expected to provide resources and protection for them. What appears to be an unusual family dynamic is actually a pretty nifty parenting hack, as studies show that 80 percent of South American Indian children with a second dad survive into adulthood, compared to 61 percent of their siblings without an extra father figure.

But let's not kid ourselves . . . the Coolidge Effect mostly just enables men to sire as many offspring as possible via widespread, short-term seed dissemination. This is not inherently bad, as Ryan reminds us that it is thanks to our male ancestors' one-track mind that we are even here. There is also another male-dominated industry where the Coolidge Effect has left a sticky residue: Internet porn.

WELCOME TO THE WONDERFUL WORLD OF PORN

If you've ever conducted a search on YouPorn, RedTube, or any of the myriad other porn sites that are now deleted from your browser history, then you know the Internet is a Wonka Factory for your Willy. Some of the most out-there genres include: vegetable porn, lactation porn, and clown porn, whose only function, as far as I can tell, is to turn you off sex completely. Teacher and founder of *YourBrainOnPorn*, Gary Wilson goes as far as to say, "Without the Coolidge Effect, there would be no Internet porn." In his viral 2012 TEDx Talk, he explained how modern porn exploits this effect, since "each novel female on a guy's screen [is viewed] as a genetic opportunity." He continued, "A guy can see more hot babes [or vegetables, nipples, or clowns] in ten minutes than his ancestors could see in several lifetimes." The value of porn is debatable. On the one hand, science confirms one hand is all it takes to reap certain benefits, from immediate gratification and stress relief to fulfillment of sexual needs and increased positivity about sex. On the flip side, a simple Google search shows nearly two million results for the phrase, "porn ruins life." And pumped into every porn-related discussion are, of course, the deleterious effects of porn addiction, which, according to multiple research journals, include depression, anger, unsatisfying sex, and anxiety. Some experts speculate delayed ejaculation and difficulty climaxing are also consequences of porn-induced "over-masturbation." Also worth noting is how men's porn overconsumption impacts women.

For the most part, it's not pretty. A 2011 *New York* magazine story recounts anecdotes of women who have either been treated like porn stars, or pretended to be porn stars in order to fulfill their man's fantasies—only to discover that men "don't want their real women and their fantasy women to inhabit the same body." In other words, women get screwed either way.

This is not to say that grown men are the only ones who get all hot and bothered watching Debbie *do* Dallas, or another Debbie, or Dallas *do* Dallas, for that matter. In 2015, *Marie Claire* surveyed 3,000 women on their porn habits and found that nearly a third of them watched porn weekly. (Ten percent tuned in daily!) Another report estimates anywhere between 20 and 50 percent of women view porn on the reg. Teenagers are watching lots of porn, too. A 2013 University of New Hampshire survey found 42 percent of ten- to seventeen-year-olds had viewed porn at least once in the past twelve months. In fact, 40 percent of fourteen- to eighteen-year-olds say they learn more about sex from porn than they do at school.

When we were kids during those pre-Internet years, Lily was one of the few kids I knew to have a coveted subscription to HBO. While the rest of us waited for those semi-annual free cable weekends, she had unlimited, unfiltered access to an amazing collection of programming 24/7. This is how, at the age of twelve, she came to discover the titillating world of late-night adult content. The first film she saw and reviewed for me was *Bar Girls*, which she described as "full-on lesbian pornography." At the time, I wasn't familiar with any lesbians or porn, so just hearing her talk about the movie felt strangely thrilling and forbidden. Years later, I would finally get to see *Bar Girls,* only to find that it had very little to do with full-on lesbian sex and more to do with chatty, lonely women looking for love in Los Angeles, kind of like a girls-only *Melrose Place*. What twelve-year-old Lily had construed as full-on sex scenes were really mild make-out sessions that even my conservative mom would be cool with today. But this is what sex education is like when the only things you learn about sex in your health class are 1) gonorrhea and 2) we shouldn't be having any.

That people, especially young people, are learning everything they know about sex from porn alarms many parents, including award-winning pornographic film-maker Erika Lust, who is a mother to two girls and the subject of an episode of *Hot Girls Wanted: Turned On,* a Netflix original documentary series co-created by Rashida Jones. It's also one of the reasons she started making feminist porn—or porn that *actually* appeals to women—which means you won't find anything but beautiful cinematography, flawless hair and makeup, and emotional, consensual sex in her erotica. Film titles and storylines also cater to the female fantasy. Take

Hysterical Piano Concert, which stars a young pianist who dreams of experiencing a mind-blowing orgasm on stage. A male character uses his talents to make her dream into a reality, but that is all. The film doesn't care about his climax. *Only hers.* This generally doesn't happen in the male-dominated, mainstream porn industry. Films like *Titty Titty Gang Bang* and *A Tale of Two Titties* suggest as much.

Whether you're watching a lady being dreamily eaten out on a piano or getting gang-banged by a dozen men, there is still something inherently dangerous about the act of watching porn. There's obviously the social taboo. And the very real possibility that one of your four roommates will walk in on you, something I was perpetually paranoid about in college when I'd stay up late watching *Hotel Erotica* reruns. For those of you who are unfamiliar with *Hotel Erotica,* you need to Google it ASAP. Each episode recycled the same ridiculous formula: a mysterious visitor arrives at the hotel and ends up seducing or being seduced by another hotel guest or employee in a fairly generic and redundant series of "love" scenes. Because it was softcore, you only got to see boobs, butts, and simulated thrusting, which was still a big deal back then. The show was terrible, but for a romantic like me, I was still transfixed, finding it equal parts arousing and anxiety-inducing.

Literary porn, like *50 Shades of Grey*, has also captivated the female mainstream with its portrayal of BDSM and romantic fantasy. By 2015, more than 125 million copies of the book had been sold worldwide, and it held the record as the fastest-selling paperback in the UK. Despite its popularity, many women still admit they are ashamed to be seen with the book—myself included.

As it turns out, this is a very normal reaction to porn, according to neuroscientists Ogi Ogas and Sai Gaddam, who cover this topic extensively in their book, *A Billion Wicked Thoughts.* They write, "Forbidden acts have a very special power to arouse . . . Both sexes can get wildly turned on by situations that are immoral or dangerous, *because* of their immorality or dangerousness." This ability to get turned on by the taboo is called a transgression cue, and because it doesn't seem to serve a clear purpose, the authors surmise "it might be a strange quirk of our brain wiring"—specifically found in our sympathetic nervous system. In addition to deciding whether we flee or fight in a scary situation, the sympathetic nervous system also controls our orgasms. In other words, the part of our brain that reacts to danger is also responsible for sexy-time urges.

In 1974, two Canadian psychologists tested this theory in the famous "love bridge" experiment, in which about eighty-five men were observed walking across either a safe, stable bridge or a wobbly, less stable bridge. As each man made their way across one of the bridges, an attractive young woman (a plant) would stop and ask him to come up with a creative story based on a photograph of a woman. She would then give him her phone number "in case he wanted to talk further." So, what happened? Apparently, fear does make you kind of horny. Fifty percent of the men who crossed the wobbly bridge called the woman, compared to just 12.5 percent of men from the stable bridge. And, the scary bridge crossers were also twice as likely to include sexual content in their creative stories than their counterparts. In a later interview, Art Aron, one of the psychologists who conducted the study, explained what happened. "If you meet someone in conditions where your heart is racing, where your body is stirred up, you're much more likely to be attracted to them."

More than thirty years later, British social scientist Paul Willis reversed the test to see if fear was the "ultimate aphrodisiac" for women as well. In a produced television segment, he recruited six women to ride a roller coaster and six other women to ride a kiddie ride at an amusement park. After they rode their respective rides, he gave all of them a list of about twenty words they could use to describe their experience. The roller coaster riders were far more likely to respond positively to words like "exhilarated," "wild," "flirty," "turned on," "naughty," and "sexy" than the women who rode the kiddie ride. Willis also tested his own pickup skills and asked each woman out for a drink afterward. Five out of the six roller coaster ladies said yes, compared to only two women from the other group.

If you think a study of twelve women doesn't sound very convincing, you're right. But what about 125 million? Earlier, I mentioned the success of *50 Shades of Grey*. Did people just quietly read the book (or more realistically, scan and skip ahead to the X-rated bits) and then try to forget it, or did they try it at home? Let's take a look at some data. The *Washington Post* reports emergency room visits have doubled since 2007—with the bulk of the increase occurring between 2012 and 2013, shortly after the release of the books. (The first book was published in 2011.) And 83 percent of the injuries required something called "foreign body removals." The adult toy industry also enjoyed a 7.5 percent bump in year-over-year growth in 2013, which some market researchers credit to the novels.

Some women have openly admitted the role the books have played in their bedroom. In her memoir, *I Like You Just the Way I Am*, the hilarious Jenny Mollen recounts their effects: "Maybe it was the graphic sex. Or the graphic sex or the graphic sex. But within two days, I was finished with the book and more sexually charged than I'd been since ever." Soon enough, she was buying sex toys like she was at a Whole Foods, eventually settling on "nipple clamps, some reasonably priced cock rings, two giant vibrators, a latex bodysuit, and a blindfold."

Findings from a 2014 study in *The Journal of Sexual Medicine* also suggest women's lust for danger and excitement in the bedroom could be contagious. Sixty-five percent of women have fantasized about being sexually dominated, 52 percent have dreamed of being tied up, and 36 percent get turned on at the thought of being spanked or whipped. Worth noting, however, is that half of the women wanted these fantasies to stay fantasies. After all, arousal is not consent.

Chapter 4
Love and . . . Breaking Up

Why the end of a relationship feels like you're being murdered.

This is how my friends describe their worst breakups.

"I'm just so sad. I've never felt like this before." —Danielle

"I'm broken. Physically broken and there's no way to put the pieces back together." —Jasmine

"I'm being suffocated by grief. I can't breathe. Everything is black." —Lily

"It's like someone stabbed me in the heart, and the life is slowly draining from my body. Nobody is coming to help me either. Because no one fucking cares." —Lisa

_____ —*You*
[fill in the blank]

Here's the bad news. The aftermath of a bad breakup is the worst part of life. It's like death, except you don't get the benefit of dying. All you do is suffer, feel sorry for yourself, or analyze everything you did or didn't do throughout the course of your entire relationship in order to figure out what the hell happened. Maybe it was him. Maybe it was you. Or, more realistically, maybe it was both of you. Unfortunately, this is all irrelevant, because IT'S OVER.

And now for some *good news*—which, I'll be frank with you, isn't all that good—but it is better than the bad news. Heartbreak, heartache, heartburn—whatever you want to call it—happens to most of us. A 2013 YouGov poll finds that 85 percent of women and 73 percent of men have had their hearts ripped out of their bodies like that very unlucky man in *Temple of Doom*. And chances are it'll happen more than once. One British study has even broken down relationships to a science, suggesting the average person will get their heart broken twice and have seven or eight relationships before finding "the one." R.E.M. sang it best: *Everybody hurts sometimes.* And the fact that many of those studied have found love again, or at the very least aren't hurting like they used to, should be very promising for the rest of us.

IT'S NOT ALL IN YOUR HEAD

In the movies, breakups are always depicted in familiar montages—quick cuts of sobbing, sappy mixtapes, bloodshot eyes, sleepless nights, and empty pints of Ben & Jerry's—reflecting reality, until a couple minutes later when the dark storm suddenly clears (typically by the serendipitous arrival of an attractive stranger), and the hole in our leading lady's (or man's) heart has suddenly been filled. In real life, this rarely happens. No good-looking stranger has ever randomly approached me post-breakup or in regular life. Where are you guys?

The pain of rejection, we are told, is all in our head, but if you have ever experienced this excruciating pain, then you know that it cuts far beyond "just feelings." As a middle child and someone who did college theater, suffice it to say I have always exhibited a penchant for melodrama, but the truth is, the resulting physical anguish I have felt from a bad breakup isn't an exaggeration. Even the American Heart Association agrees a broken heart can *literally* break your heart. Stress-induced cardiomyopathy, better known as broken heart syndrome, can cause shortness of breath and intense chest pain (similar to a heart attack), caused by an overload of stress hormones, like cortisol and adrenaline, which are released in times of extreme emotional duress. This trauma temporarily enlarges your heart and stymies the blood flow to your heart, which, under the right conditions, can kill you. And because this condition is sexist, it happens more often to women.

A bad breakup can also break your brain. In 2010, researchers at Rutgers University conducted a study of people who had been recently dumped but were still madly in love with their exes. Instead of putting their heads in the oven, these sad saps opted for an MRI machine and were shown pictures of their exes. The scans showed that heartbroken brains closely resembled those of drug addicts going through cocaine withdrawal. Not surprising considering that love is just as (if not more) addictive than cocaine, as both are tied to our brain's primitive reward system. Each time we get a hit of the good stuff, our brains get a jolt of dopamine, a chemical that activates feelings of intense pleasure. Which explains why going through withdrawal of any kind results in such a huge shock to the system. It's like one moment you're sipping piña coladas on a tropical beach in the Caribbean; the next, you're locked up in a padded prison cell and wearing maxi pads as shower shoes. Is it any wonder why heartbreak drives people to depression, suicide, or texting their exes twenty-six times in two minutes?

What's more, our brains aren't sophisticated enough to differentiate between pain from social rejection and pain from, say, a sucker punch to the face. In yet another study where brokenhearted saps were tortured with photos of their exes, brain scans revealed that seeing these photos activated the same areas of the brain that are associated with physical or sensory pain. And if your relationship was serious (e.g., living together, considering marriage), you can expect the pain to be more intense. Imagine making huge financial, emotional, and psychological investments in your partner, only to have your entire account suddenly wiped out. Having children only adds to the agony, as you must now navigate the world as a newly stressed-out single parent, struggling with unfamiliar time and financial demands, all while trying to maintain a non-hostile relationship with an ex who you may have complicated feelings toward, whether it be homicidal, reconciliatory, or somewhere in between. Interestingly, one breakup pain buffer, according to the results of a comprehensive, twenty-month post-breakup study of a thousand adults, were happy relationships. While it sounds counterintuitive, researchers found people who were satisfied during their relationships fared better when they were over than their counterparts who were in rockier pairings. The theory here is that people in positive relationships are generally positive people, a character trait that comes in handy during difficult or stressful situations.

YOU REALLY CAN GET OVER A BREAKUP

Researchers say it takes about three months to get over a breakup, unless you're me . . . or Taylor Swift. My final breakup with Joe left me so damaged that I quit my job, applied to grad school, cashed in my savings, and flew to Nepal to volunteer at an orphanage, hoping to bypass the *Eat* and *Pray* part of my life and fast-forward straight to *Love*. (I know Elizabeth Gilbert went to Bali, but the flight to Nepal was cheaper.)

Starting a new life in a different country is an effective way to have a fresh start and put your troubles in perspective. Had I stayed in my rut in Los Angeles, I would have wallowed in fear and misery indefinitely, stuffing my face with Indian takeout that would give me stomachaches and praying for Joe's return. But Nepal changed everything. It was during my time there that I was accepted into an editorial internship program at *Psychology Today,* where I first started writing about relationships. Unlike Gilbert, I didn't find love, but for those precarious few months I wasn't consumed by my breakup, which was almost as rewarding.

Traveling to faraway and exotic destinations to get over heartbreak and hardship are not as accessible now that I have no savings, but, through the years, I have learned to let go of lament in other simpler and cheaper ways. Namely with these following phrases:

1. *I love myself.* Cheeseball. I know. But it works, especially if you believe it. Those who practice self-love and self-compassion are less prone to depression and anxiety, and are generally happier and more optimistic, according to numerous studies and common sense. Loving yourself is also empowering, according to self-help guru (he knows Oprah!) Mastin Kipp, who writes on his website, TheDailyLove.com, self-love is crucial "because ultimately we are the ones responsible for our actions, choices, and the outcome of those actions and choices. We cannot give to someone else what we don't have, and likewise we cannot get from someone else what he or she doesn't have." If you love yourself, *you* will be the master of your feelings, not some idiot who broke your heart via text message.

2. *I want to be happy.* Seriously, do you? This seems like a dumb question. Of course I want to be happy, who doesn't? The problem is, a lot of the time, I actually don't. I allow minor offensive actions to stage a coup d'état over my common sense. My grudges span decades. I still haven't forgiven that little shit Richard O., who spent all of fourth grade taunting me by calling me *Jenny Craig.* Los Angeles parking enforcement officials are also familiar with my unforgiving vengeance, as they have been on the receiving end of numerous nasty contest letters for unfairly issued parking tickets. In these situations, I couldn't care less about happiness; rather, I am singularly focused on seeking justice or proving that I am, in fact, in the right. (Which I am!) But being right oftentimes does not culminate in content. Now when I am on the verge of getting worked up, I try to stop and remind myself that my end goal is joy. I might even put my teeth together and force a smile, because, as it turns out, even a fake grin is better than none at all, according to researchers at the University of Kansas, who found

holding your mouth in a smiling position could help decrease your heart rate after a stressful situation.

3. *Fuck him/her.* I'm not a big fan of cursing, especially since I joined the No Cussing Club back in 2008 (although this book will probably get me kicked out of that shit), but fucked-up language might actually be good for you, finds a study published in the journal *NeuroReport.* "Swearing may serve an important function in relieving pain." Say it, whisper it, scream it—let it all out. Not only are you soothing the pain, you are also telling yourself that you are not going to be a victim.

4. *I always hated his dumb haircut.* Remember that annoying thing about your ex that always bothered you but you refused to admit because you were so *madly in love?* Well, it's time to dish the dirt. Take off your love goggles and tell yourself what you really saw in him. Even if it's something as tiny as I hated his pinky toenails, embrace it. Doing so will help you realize that your ex wasn't as fabulous or perfect as he/she seemed, and it will help you heal faster. In fact, researchers at the University of Utah found that those who "indicated strong negative feelings about their ex in the immediate aftermath of the breakup were less likely to be depressed."

5. *I am better off without him or her, because . . .* Quick! Finish the sentence. For me, it was: I am better off without him because now I can finally eat blueberries! At the time, my ex had a terrible allergy to the fruit (which just happens to be one of my favorites). He wouldn't kiss me or come near me if I had eaten anything blueberry flavored, so, eventually, I stopped eating them. The first thing I did after our breakup was devour a pint of blueberries. Obviously, they didn't do much to change how I felt (other than turning my teeth blue), but there was a small sense of relief, being able to enjoy something that I couldn't have when we were together. And during a breakup, that's the only feeling you should be striving for.

6. *It has been x days since we broke up, and I feel . . .* Here's another fill-in-the-blank for you. You can say whatever you like, just be truthful. If you'd rather write it down in a journal, that's okay, too. The reason I like this phrase is that it keeps you present in the current moment and lets you feel whatever it is you need to feel. Eventually, one day will turn into thirty days, and

you will notice a difference. You may still be miserable, but just like any physical wound, the degree to which you feel the pain will lessen over time. And even if it doesn't feel like anything is getting better, the findings from one UCLA study suggest otherwise. Naming your feelings (even the awful ones) reduces sadness, anger, and pain, says study author and psychology professor Matthew D. Lieberman. "When you put feelings into words, you're activating this prefrontal region [the part of the brain that helps process emotions] and seeing a reduced response in the amygdala [the part of the brain associated with feelings of fear and danger]. In the same way you hit the brake when you're driving when you see a yellow light, when you put feelings into words, you seem to be hitting the brakes on your emotional responses."

7. *I will find someone better.* These words are probably the most difficult to say, particularly if you believed that your ex was "the one." Trust me, we've all been there. (It's basically the reason you're reading this book.) And because this phrase is so hard to say, it is the most crucial. In fact, not saying it can and will prolong your misery. When researchers at Stanford University analyzed hundreds of breakup stories, they found that those who saw themselves as victims or blamed the demise of their relationship on themselves had a harder time moving on post-breakup than those who chalked up their splits to circumstances outside of their control, such as timing or location. Giving up on love or greeting everyone you meet with a "Hi, how are you? Did you know that I'm going to die alone and miserable?" also sets you up for a self-fulfilling prophecy, which countless studies have confirmed is real.

EVERYTHING STILL HURTS AND I WANT TO DIE. (SO WHY IS HE OK?)

Food poisoning is the worst, but it's slightly more bearable when you are retching next to someone you love. There's something comforting about holding each other's hair while you take turns on the toilet and sips of 7UP. There is a unique intimacy in this shared misery, one that I expect to find in the aftermath of a gruesome breakup. Of course your ex is suffering as much as you, right? So why does this dum-dum's Instagram suddenly look like it's been hacked by the cast of *Entourage,* while you're paralyzed in a fetal position on the bathroom floor?

I want to be clear that there are no set rules or regulations when it comes to experiencing a breakup. Based on my own experience and observations, however, I have found that, in general, men seem to be blessed with a faster recovery time. One reason for this may be that men simply do not compute pain the same way women do. Neuroscientists at Georgia State University studied pain regions in the brain and found that women suffer higher incidences of severe or chronic pain than men. Because microglia—the brain's immune cells—tend to be more active in women, they may require nearly twice the dosage of pain-relief medication than men. Though this study isn't necessarily related to breakup anguish, it does support the argument that men and women process pain differently.

This is not to say that men emerge unscathed after a split. *Not at all.* When researchers at Binghamton University surveyed more than 5,000 people from ninety-six countries, they concluded that breaking up sucks for all parties involved. On a graded scale, men were generally found to experience less pain—both emotional and physical—than women after a breakup, but it didn't necessarily mean they were less invested than their partners. This attitude isn't personal. It's biology. Lead researcher Craig Morris explains: "From a biological perspective, women bear the larger minimum parental investment—nine months of gestation as well as the metabolic costs of lactation—and therefore are more 'selective' in their mate choice." In short, our current behavior is still largely shaped by our evolutionary ancestors who needed not just any man, but a mighty, mighty good man, who could provide for her and her children for the long term. So you can imagine how devastating it is to have him unsubscribe from her mating list.

If there is any silver lining to this suffering, it is that women are better equipped to handle it. To combat depression, women will find solace in their friends and practice constructive strategies for healing, including trying to (not obsessively) analyze what went wrong in the relationship, which provides long-term benefits. In one collegiate study, Morris found that while women lost more self-esteem after a breakup (twice as much as men), they were able to reap increased personal awareness and greater perceptivity regarding future relationships, which ultimately helped them recover more fully and emerge emotionally stronger than men. However, talking things out does have its limits, as any good friend and researcher will tell you. Studies of adolescents indicate that many girls are at risk of "excessive problem talk," which exacerbates depression and anxiety.

Another reason women may have a rougher time with a breakup is that it's what's expected of them. On *Psychology Today*, psychologist Melanie Greenberg suggests that women tend to "obsess or ruminate" about their exes because they "have been socialized to take more responsibility for relationships, leading to more time spent thinking about what went wrong or what they could have done differently." For most men, self-reflection is not on the menu. Rather, they channel their heartbreak through anger and engaging in self-destructive behaviors (e.g., getting piss drunk and partying every night) to preserve their self-esteem. Scott Carroll, a relationship expert and psychiatrist at the University of New Mexico, told me: "Men tend to repress their grieving and take a fake-it-until-you-make-it approach . . . some men become dogs and go for every hookup . . . but they are terrified of intimacy and run like hell if a woman wants anything more." Unable to confront their feelings, he says men will drown their sorrows in their career, hobbies, or going out—literally anything to keep their mind off their loss and pain.

Maybe it's time to reconsider those happy Instagram posts after all? The reality is, according to science, it takes men *longer* to get over a breakup than women. It can take years, even decades, for men to get over their heartbreak, says Carroll. "They just don't show their grief to others—or even to themselves." In fact, the worse the pain, the more they have to hide it. In many cultures, men are raised to believe sensitivity is weakness, vulnerability is defeat, and feelings are bad. And even though women are more likely to attempt suicide, men are four times more likely to die by suicide, as their methods tend to be more violent and lethal. Why this is the case is uncertain, but a 2015 *Guardian* newspaper article suggests "men are more intent on dying" based on a 2005 British study, which found self-harming men reported considerably higher levels of suicidal intent than self-harming women. There's also the fact that some men simply find talking about their problems a "waste of time," a sentiment also shared by the boys in the previous study. It could be because "talking about problems will make the problems feel bigger," explained Dr. Amanda J. Rose, one of the study's authors.

Hormones also play a role in expediting breakup pain for men. Biologist Dawn Maslar told me that when a man enters a relationship, his testosterone levels drop, making him more susceptible to bonding with oxytocin—the hormone that makes you feel all stupidly lovey-dovey. Once he decides to call the relationship quits, however, his testosterone levels shoot back up, offsetting the effects of oxytocin, so that he literally stops feeling the love. In other words, says Maslar, "when he's done, he's done, because his body helps him to disconnect." Research studies further suggest that men with higher levels of testosterone are more likely to break up with their partners. Human men aren't the only ones to suffer from testosterone overload. Species of birds, like the monogamous, loyal male sparrows, when injected with testosterone, turn into adulterous, deadbeat dads, leaving their nests to hook up with other chicks. It's also no coincidence that many newly single men find themselves stepping up their gym game; after all, exercise is one of the most effective ways to naturally increase testosterone levels. Still, this sex hormone is primarily a young man's game. By the time they hit their thirties, some men begin to lose around 10 percent of their testosterone every decade. Women also produce testosterone, but in far lower quantities than men.

THE BEST WAY TO GET OVER A BREAKUP IS . . .

Many best friends, whether fictionalized in a romantic comedy or in real-life, say the same thing: *To get over a breakup, get under someone else.* As it turns out, rebound is the most effective way to distract yourself from your heartbreak and also prove to yourself that there is, in fact, life after the death of a relationship. Several studies have found that dating someone new is one of the best ways to mitigate breakup woes—even casual rebound relationships help people feel more confident and desirable after heartbreak. And the faster you get it on with someone new, the faster you'll be referring to your ex as "who?"

One 2009 collegiate study found that simply thinking optimistically about a nonexistent future relationship was enough to expedite the recovery process. Researchers split up unattached adult participants—all who had experienced a breakup—into two groups. One group was asked to read a magazine article that promoted a positive attitude toward breaking up and cited cheery made-up statistics, like: 87 percent of people report being happier and more satisfied with new partners than their past ones. The other group was asked to read an article with a more pessimistic tone and that included more depressing predictions, such as: 87 percent of people say there is simply no one good enough to date. Afterward, participants were questioned about their previous relationships. Researchers found the optimism-conditioned group were more likely to offer a hopeful view of their next relationship and decreased attachment to their exes than those in the pessimism-conditioned study. In other words, *Inception*-style idea harvesting totally works—and you don't even have to be asleep for it to happen.

A note about rebounding: A rebound relationship doesn't necessarily require sex—but it is often a part of many of these relationships. According to a survey published in the journal *Archives of Sexual Behavior,* up to one-third of college coeds have engaged in a rebound romp in the bedroom within a month of a previous relationship's demise. And it's usually the hurt and angry dumpees who are the most likely to partake in revenge sex against their exes. Though, how much pain or spite your ex will feel from said revenge sex is unclear.

BUT I WANT HIM BACK . . .

Me too. Sometimes it hurts so bad you convince yourself that you'd be willing to do anything to get back with this person. Maybe this means getting Brazilian waxes every week, or agreeing to support him and his fledgling music career, or telling yourself that his reluctance to commit to you is actually true love. So this is what happens: You send a text (or reply to one of his). And then you stalk his social media profiles for most of the workday. Or if you're old-school, you'll drive/walk/bike/crawl past his house a few dozen times, when you know he'll be home. Or maybe you'll get completely shit-faced and show up at his doorstep in the middle of the night, then beg to be let in like a stray dog and unsuccessfully try to seduce him—only to wake up the next morning alone on the floor, covered in puke and pity. If that isn't love, I don't know what is.

Let's try to unpack how we got here, shall we? First, the primal, unadulterated joy we get from seeing his name appear on our phone (or in the restraining order he's filed against us) is caused by an intoxicating hit of dopamine, which you might recall is a feel-good chemical that transforms us into bloodthirsty vampires on the hunt for pleasure. Brain scans of recently dumped people show that looking at pictures of their exes actually releases dopamine. You may be thinking, *Hey, what's wrong with having a dopamine rush? It sounds good to me!* It may feel good now, but the effects are only temporary and highly addictive . . . like scary addictive. Not to mention another unintended consequence of dopamine is that it maniacally shifts your desire for the object of your affection into extreme overdrive, which is probably not the best idea, considering you guys are broken up and he might never want to see your beautiful face again.

But the truth is, many people get back together with their exes. One acquaintance broke up with her boyfriend after he refused to propose to her. Three months later, they got back together, got engaged shortly after, and now are happily married with two adorable children. Another woman I know broke up with her first love shortly after college, married someone else, got divorced, then rekindled the relationship with her first love more than a decade later. They are one of the happiest couples I know—at least according to their social media.

Relationship recycling, in fact, has become remarkably common, due in large part to society's growing acceptance of casual sex and ambiguous in-between couplings. One 2009 study at the University of Texas found that 65 percent of college coeds have gotten back together after a breakup. A separate 2013 study conducted by researchers at the University of Kansas found that 37 percent of cohabitating couples and 23 percent of married couples reconciled after a split. Plenty of other studies reveal additional promising statistics that are bound to instill hope in those who wish to reunite with their exes. There's just one little wrinkle: *Your ex must also be game.* In general, researchers say men are more likely to try to win back their exes than women whereas older, educated women tend to make their relationship exits permanent.

BUT WHY DID HE BREAK UP WITH ME?

Who shot Tony Soprano? Who killed JFK? Is the dress white and gold or black and blue? Will we ever know the answers to these mysteries? Likely not. But we must somehow find a way to live our lives anyway.

WILL I EVER FIND CLOSURE?

There is something wholly intoxicating about the idea of closure. *We want it. We need it. We are owed it!* We expect closure will magically grant us with a life-affirming epiphany or cinematic catharsis usually reserved for the movies. We put such value and hope in getting closure, that on the rare occasion we do get it, we often don't accept it, because it's usually not the closure we imagined. So we try to order another round of closure from the universe—one that works for us. But by then, the universe has moved on, even if we haven't.

That one time I did get closure from a relationship, it was a real letdown. Charles and I had remained friendly after the breakup, even though privately I harbored reservations about why we broke up. He had come to the conclusion that it wouldn't work because we would be in different countries, despite my protests that we could make long-distance work. In hindsight, it was clear that he no longer wanted to be in a relationship with me and used our distance as a convenient scapegoat. Years later, I half-jokingly confronted him about what had transpired all those years ago. He was surprisingly receptive and candidly explained that while he loved me, we were in our early twenties and still had so much to experience in the world. He thought that we wouldn't be able to fully experience our lives had we stayed together. A better, more mature person might feel satisfied by this answer, but I was left feeling more confused. The hopeless romantic in me couldn't understand why he thought that us being together would somehow prevent us from experiencing the world. He had given me closure, but not the kind I wanted. The kind I wanted, needed, and felt I was owed involved him confessing that he made a terrible, life-destroying mistake by letting me go, and each day without me was filled with regret, longing, and insurmountable agony.

This kind of closure—or any closure for that matter—doesn't exist, according to Nancy Berns, a sociologist and author of *Closure: The Rush to End Grief and What It Costs Us.* She describes closure as a social construct or "frame used to explain how we should respond to loss." It's how culture tells us we should feel or react to tragedy. One of the first times she heard the word "closure" used in popular culture was on the sitcom *Friends*, when recently single Rachel left a boozy message on Ross's voicemail, announcing: "I am over you. And that, my friend, is what they call closure." In the end, however, Rachel doesn't find closure—evidenced by the couple's multi-season cycle of getting back together and breaking up—and neither do we.

Another problem with closure is that it only works in the parameters of a just world, which, as we should know by now, also does not exist. To have the person who broke your heart explain why he did it, take responsibility for hurting you, and tell you that he's truly, deeply sorry—these kinds of scenarios don't happen in the real world. Speaking of other scenarios that don't happen in the real world . . .

Chapter 5
Love and . . . "The One"

Why we will never, ever find our soul mate.

The first human to dream up the existence of soul mates was the Greek philosopher Plato, who based this theology on Egyptian mythology. In *The Symposium*, he purports early humans were pretty much born as conjoined twins, each of us with four arms, four legs, and one head with two faces. But these octo-humans were so awesome that Zeus started to feel threatened by their power. He decided to split them up into two parts (the male and the female) and separate them so they would spend their lives looking for their other half, hence the popularity of the phrase "you complete me," found in many self-written wedding vows. Aside from making Zeus look like a totally paranoid dictator, this soul mate theory has also convinced many lonely people throughout history that successfully finding your other half is the ultimate test and proof of true love.

But like with any test where you haven't mastered the subject material, you are bound to be rudely schooled by everything you don't know. Namely, soul mate theory can seriously twist and limit your perspective on relationships, leaving you trapped in situations that are unhealthy, mediocre, dangerous, or all of the above. When my friend Lucy found the man she thought she was going to marry, she was unable to see how destructive her relationship was. For years, I listened to her detail terrifying instances of physical and verbal abuse and violence, yet each time I begged her to leave him, she defended her decision to stay. He was *the love of her life*, after all.

What might have also exacerbated Lucy's unrelenting devotion to this relationship was her aversion to sunk costs. As the name implies, sunk costs refer to all the money, time, and energy invested in a relationship that can never be recouped. If you've ever been to Vegas, then you know that most people don't deal well with losing. After a string of folds at the poker table, the common sense response might be to walk away with the meager amount of cash and dignity you have left, but many gamblers will continue playing—investing even more money, time, and energy into the same bad situation in the hopes that it will miraculously work out in their favor. This is called the sunk cost fallacy, and to many hopeless romantics and soul mate subscribers, it's our worst enemy.

Why can't we just cut our losses even when it's pretty clear we're already knee-deep in crap? "The problem is one of focus," writes social psychologist Heidi Grant Halvorson in *The Atlantic*. "We worry far too much about what we'll lose if we just move on, instead of focusing on the costs of *not* moving on: more wasted time and effort, more unhappiness, and more missed opportunities."

Other conditions also entice us to stay. A 2016 study in *Current Psychology* found that people were more willing to overlook their own needs and remain in unhappy relationships if they had purchased a house together or if it seemed like their partner was making an effort to improve the relationship.

And there is another downside to soul mate theory, which is that it can hold your partner to an absurdly high and unrealistic standard where no one wins. In one 2014 study, individuals in long-term partnerships were primed to think about their relationships in the context of a perfect unity (e.g., we're made for each other) or journey (e.g. we've been through a lot). The participants were then asked to recall either a fight or celebration they had experienced with their partners and rate how satisfied they were in their relationships. You might assume that those who were asked to recall fights would be more likely to report less content relationship statuses, but this was only true for participants from the perfect unity group. None of this surprises me. The onus of being in a perfect relationship is that nothing can be imperfect, which explains why the journey mind-set group was not burdened with the expectation of a flawless relationship. They evaluated the health of their relationship not on individual memories, but through the lens of a holistic, evolving progression.

SOUL MATES ON-SCREEN

There is very little scientific evidence or proof supporting the existence of soul mates, yet it is a consistent mainstay of almost every fictionalized romance. On-screen, convincing portrayals of love at first sight are proof that each person is just waiting to find their *one*. But is it real? According to evolutionary biologist and love guru Helen Fisher, instantaneous love is not only possible, it is an essential aspect of the mating game. She calls it a "basic mammalian response that is developed in other animals and our ancestors to speed up the mating process."

But it doesn't happen to just everyone. Men, who are generally more visually stimulated, feel this romantic impulse more than women. Fisher isn't the first scientist to make this hopelessly romantic claim. In her book, *Why We Love*, she recalls an observation by Charles Darwin as he witnessed a romance unfold between two ducks: "It was evidently a case of love at first sight, for she swam about the newcomer caressingly . . . with overtures of affection." Though instant love is genuine, Fisher admits that it doesn't always last forever. In the animal kingdom, infatuation can last anywhere from a few seconds to a few weeks. Still, she argues that there is nothing more powerful than our desire for love. Back in 2009, she and her team of researchers studied the brains of forty-nine people who were madly in love through a brain scanner and discovered "the most dramatic activity occurs in the 'reward system,' the 'wanting' system, the brain system that gives lovers their focus, energy, ecstasy, and motivation to seek life's greatest prize, a mating partner." Attraction also activates this brain system.

Though I am not sure if I have ever felt true love at first sight, I have certainly succumbed to crazy, stupid, love syndrome, in which I justify bad decisions and romantic delusions by claiming *it's love, so it's A-OK!*, a bad habit I picked up from my favorite characters in television and the movies.

For six excruciating seasons between 1998 and 2004, *Sex and the City*'s Carrie Bradshaw swung pendulously from Big to [insert random celebrity guest star] until finally confirming that Big was, indeed, "the one" in the series finale. Women collectively were relieved by this predictably happy ending, until, of course, the show became a movie franchise, and Big ostensibly returns to his dickish ways, leaving poor haute-coutured Carrie at the altar. In a pathetic attempt to win her back, he sends her a lot of plagiarized spam, to which her Stockholm syndrome kicks in and she declares, "It wasn't logic, it was love," before leaping back into his arms.

But this isn't logic or love; it is an idealized version of what romance is supposed to be, one that books and movies have been pimping out since the days of Shakespeare. These are timeless stories that appeal to every generation. Every year there seems to be a revival or remake of a Shakespearean classic. *Romeo and Juliet* is the second-most adapted of his plays; nearly forty depictions of these star-crossed lovers have splashed across the silver screen over the past century.

For the most part, cinematic and literary romance follows a generic formula: Boy meets girl. Boy falls in love with girl. Hijinks ensue, which prevent them from being together, until twinkle music starts to play on-screen, and then they miraculously find a way to get back together. *The End*. Nothing stops these couples from returning to their soul mates—"not even death can stop true love," which is a direct line from one of the best film romances of all time, *The Princess Bride*.

On the rare occasion that predestined soul mates do not reach the happily-ever-after portion of the film, people get pissed. In *La La Land*—the 2016 magical romantic-comedy musical about artsy hipsters falling in love in Hollywood—soul mates Sebastian and Mia *(spoiler alert)* do not end up together. Instead, the audience is taunted by a series of dreamy, hypothetical vignettes, depicting *what could've been*: their perfect, storybook courtship, wedding, home, and family. That the film betrayed the destiny of these soul mates was heartbreaking to some viewers, like *IndieWire.com's* Kate Erbland, who describes the surprise ending as "such a gut-wrenching twist after everything the pair had been through." For others, like my friend Lily, it was infuriating.

"I hated it. I FUCKING HATED it" was her no-holds-barred review, which she admits was determined solely by the film's last five minutes. Interestingly, I didn't hate it at all. In fact, I loved it and found it to be one of the most refreshingly honest takes on love.

Sebastian and Mia had every opportunity to stay in touch with each other during the five years they were apart. It wasn't as if she was on Mars. Her film was shooting in Paris, which is far away, yes, but can also be conveniently reached by airplane or Snapchat. In a typical romantic comedy, the leading couple is kept apart by an uncontrollable outside circumstance. They want to be together, but one of them is already attached or has a terrible secret from their past. *La La Land's* leads, however, exercised agency throughout the entire film. They made every decision because they thought it was the right thing for them. And, in the end, they both decided that pursuing their career aspirations had a better payoff than pursuing each other. In other words, they still got their happy endings. That they didn't end up together doesn't necessarily undermine the authenticity or quality of their relationship. That final meaningful gaze they share in the film suggests as much. In other words, it was both *love and logic*.

In chapter one, I speculated that Disney romance might have shaped the mind-sets of fragile and impressionable minds like my own. But some research suggests that even mature adult minds can be influenced by what they see on the screen. In one 2008 study at Heriot-Watt University, participants were split into two groups: one watched the romantic comedy *Serendipity*, while the other saw a David Lynch film. (For those of you unfamiliar with *Serendipity*, the 2001 rom-com stars a charming John Cusack and Kate Beckinsale who meet one day by chance and hit it off, but ultimately decide that if they're really supposed to be together, fate will bring them together once again. There is no movie I love to hate-watch more than this film.) When the study participants were interviewed afterward, the *Serendipity* watchers reported being more likely to believe in fate and destiny than those who had watched the Lynch film. In another study, researchers found that the majority of problems plaguing real-life couples in counseling were misconceptions related to commonly romanticized film tropes, such as the belief that if a partner really loved you, then they would know what you were thinking, or that everyone has a predestined soul mate. Blaming movies for our own actions and behaviors can take us down a slippery slope, however. The charged debate of whether violent movies and video games make people more violent continues to rage, with vocal supporters on both sides.

Even if movies don't turn us into full-fledged violent killers or soul-mate-hunting zombies, they can still have a profound effect on our psyche. In one *A Clockwork Orange*-inspired study, researchers found that repeated exposure to films can change our morals. For the experiment, test subjects watched either a romance film or an action flick and were later interviewed. The resulting conversations indicated that the romance film watchers were far more sensitive, fair, respectful, and empathetic toward others than their action film counterparts. Which suggests the more we see art imitate the cruel realities of life—depressing and unsettling as it might be—the better we will be at tempering our own quixotic expectations. The relationships depicted in HBO's *Girls* are filled with excellent examples of romantic verisimilitude. In striking contrast to *Sex and the City*'s technicolor, high-fashion world of idealized romance, *Girls* offers a perspective on relationships and friendships so gritty, dark, and off-putting, that it has earned critical acclaim for its realistic portrayal of unlikeable, yet relatable millennials. When she initially pitched the show to HBO, a twenty-three-year-old Lena Dunham said she wanted to create characters based on real people. "They're beautiful and maddening. They're self-aware and self-obsessed. They're your girlfriends and daughters and sisters and employees. They're my friends, and I've never seen them on TV."

DOES "THE ONE" EVEN EXIST?

In a refreshingly candid 2016 op-ed for *The New York Times*, titled "Why You Will Marry the Wrong Person," British philosopher Alain de Botton explains why there is no such thing as *the one*. "We seem normal only to those who don't know us very well," he wrote, referring to our tendency to put on our best behavior when we meet someone. We smile and laugh way more than usual. If you're me, you pretend to like sports and drinking PBR. We do not let our guard down or reveal our strange, potentially annoying quirks and behaviors (e.g., farting in your sleep or always leaving the last bite of something) that others might find disgusting or bizarre, but to us are cute and endearing. We continue this charade until we are able to convince ourselves and our partners that we are right for each other, so we dive into marriage and hope for the best, even though we don't really know or understand each other's complexities at all.

And even in marriage, what we are seeking is not happiness, but familiarity. Botton adds, "We are looking to create, within our adult relationships, the feelings we knew so well in childhood." Feelings, which much of the time, are left over from the negative relationship dynamics of our past (e.g., I never felt my parents showed me enough affection or I never felt like I was allowed to express my needs or wants.) This thinking, he explains, is why we attract people who are wrong for us, or worse, exactly like our parents. "We marry the wrong people because we don't associate being loved with feeling happy."

The implausibility of finding, let alone marrying, exactly the right person, is also supported by the scientific community through the Fermi Paradox. Named after nuclear physicist Enrico Fermi, the paradox attempts to reconcile the contradiction between the lack of evidence and the high probability of alien life. Long, complicated story short: there are lots of stars, and even more planets (think in the trillions) in the galaxy, many of which (about 52,000) have been calculated by the Drake Equation (a fancy equation we'll discuss later) to be older than Earth, which means they should theoretically have the capacity to sustain life, as well as have figured out space travel (like us). So why haven't we gotten into even one fender bender on the intergalactic highway? Where is everybody? Does our solar system smell bad? Are they playing hard to find? Or are they already here and just hiding in plain sight—a plot ripped out of the '90s hit show *Roswell?*

These are the same questions that lonely people, myself included, have asked throughout millennia. If there's seven billion of us in the world, why is it so difficult to find someone who wants to love me the way I want them to? *Where is my soul mate?* Apparently, scientists took all this whining literally and turned to the Drake Equation to calculate the number of soul mates that a person might have, which looks something like this:

target population x % of target gender x % of single people x % of single people that you will likely run into (you probably would not randomly meet Leonardo DiCaprio at Costco) x % of target age range x % who speak a common language x % of people you find attractive x % of people who find you attractive = number of soul mates!

In an episode of the delightfully named PBS series, *It's Okay to Be Smart,* scientists use the above formula to figure out that the average twenty-five-year-old single woman in New York City has about 871 perfect partners out there. At first glance, 871 is a wildly impressive number, but this number only represents the number of people that you *might* want to date, not necessarily fall head over heels in love with. Once you account for important soul mate variables, such as a shared love for *Arrested Development* or a mutual dislike of Rachel in accounting, the pool shrinks further. The more x factors you require, the slimmer the pickings, and thus the more difficult it becomes to find *the one.*

Further investigations into soul mate science also reveal dire results. While the above example represents a liberal, hippie commune approach to soul mates, in that there can be many right ones for you, Randall Munroe, a former NASA roboticist and the founder of the popular webcomic xkcd.com, adheres to a more conservative definition, meaning there is only one *the one.* He explained that to calculate the odds of finding that one special person in the entire history of the world who was made just for you, you must first accept some harsh truths. Namely, there's a very good chance your soul mate is dead, since the current world population only represents about 10 percent of the entire human population that has ever been alive. *Remember,* you only have one soul mate in the history of the world. On the other hand, we can't discount the fact that our soul mate hasn't been born yet either, since the future is still, you know, in the future.

But let's put aside those pesky logical fallacies for a minute and pretend your one and only is currently alive and age appropriate (as to avoid any *To Catch a Predator*-related felonies). According to Munroe, the size of most people's soul mate pool comes to half a billion potential matches. While this is an enormous number, the likelihood of us actually meeting any of these people is infinitesimally small.

Think about how many different people you meet or talk to, hell, even make eye contact with on a given day. Most days, for me at least, the number is three, with one of those people being me, looking at myself in the mirror.

But let's say you're not a social pariah/hermit, and you actually make eye contact with thirty people every day, and 10 percent of those people are within your appropriate age range. That means you'll have seen three potential partners per day, about 100 people per month, or 1,200 people per year. In the span of a lifetime, assuming you don't get cataracts, you will have crossed paths with up to 80,000 people. That still comes out to less than .016 percent of your total soul mate pool, which means the chances of you finding your other half is 1.6 times out of every 10,000 lifetimes. *Good luck!*

BUT I STILL WANT MY SOUL MATE, DAMNIT!

Just because scientific theories don't have any faith in soul mate theory doesn't mean that it's not true, right? After all, everyone knows someone who ended up with their soul mate. And if you don't, just read the "about" section of any mommy blog. These outlier situations are known as exceptions to the rule, a concept popularized in the 2004 bestselling self-help book, *He's Just Not That Into You*, by Greg Behrendt and Liz Tuccillo, two *Sex and the City* writing alums. Most relationships follow a set of generally established rules:

- If a guy doesn't call, he doesn't like you.
- If a guy doesn't ask you out, he doesn't like you.
- If a guy tells you he doesn't like you, he doesn't like you.

By following and accepting these rules, we can help our relationships die with some form of dignity. The problem occurs when we delude ourselves into believing we are an exception:

- He didn't call, but I know he likes me.
- He didn't ask me out, but I know he really wants to.
- He told me he never wants to see me again, but I'm pretty sure he's going to propose!

On one hand, these delusions of grandeur help to protect our fragile egos, but on the other, they are alternative facts with no basis in reality.

Science finds millennials are the most susceptible to this *exceptional* thinking. The largest generational group in history, born in the 1980s and 1990s, we grew up with parents, teachers, and Mr. Rogers regularly reminding us of how special we are and how we deserve everything, instilling in us an overblown sense of self-confidence and entitlement. Millennials are now labeled the most narcissistic, lazy, fame-obsessed, and developmentally stunted generation *ever*. Forty percent of us believe we should get promoted every two years, regardless of our work performance. One 2007 survey found that adolescent girls are three times more likely to dream of becoming a celebrity's personal assistant than a senator. And these traits are shared by millennials across all income brackets and cultures. In fact, a writer for *Forbes* described China's one-child policy, which formally ended in 2015, as giving birth to a generation of "emperors and empresses" who grew up being the "center of the universe." Today they are privileged, entitled, and "enjoy a good life," and intend for things to stay this way.

You can see how this expectation for special treatment might emerge into other facets of our lives. Millennials were bred to expect VIP access to all the finer things in life, so why would we want to settle for average love when we could have a soul mate?

Chapter 6
Love and . . . Countdowns, Ultimatums, and Other Questionable Power Moves

Why it's probably a bad idea to threaten someone into marriage.

FADE IN:

EXTERIOR STREET—NIGHT

Police cars are parked in front of a city apartment building. The flashers swirl ominous designs on the building's facade. Worried police officers talk to each other in hushed tones. A crowd of anxious onlookers has gathered to watch the scene unfold. The tension grows as a man (early fifties) wearing a tactical vest—FBI strewn across the front—paces back and forth. But then . . .

RING RING RING! The Nokia ringtone from the late '90s sounds off in the agent's pocket. A few police officers attempt to stifle a giggle, not realizing that the ringtone was still available. Others are too young to recognize the ringtone as a thing, so they watch, bewildered. Ignoring them, the agent tightens his grip on the phone and tentatively puts it to his ear.

AGENT RICK JOHNSON (into the phone): Jen. Please, don't do anything drastic.

A muffled woman's voice can be heard on the line, but barely. Agent Johnson nods, signaling to one of the officers to get something to write on.

AGENT JOHNSON: You're telling me you guys are still OK? You're together? No, I'm not doubting you. Jen, I believe you. You don't want to hurt anyone. I know.

Ripe beads of sweat begin to drip from the agent's forehead. This is the last thing he wants to be doing. The officer returns and hands him a legal pad and pencil.

AGENT JOHNSON: OK. I have a pencil and paper. Now, tell me your demands. What's it going to take to get you and everyone else out of this situation in one piece?

More muffled sounds, interspersed with crying, can be heard on the line. Agent Johnson shakes his head as he begins to write something on the legal pad. Defeated, he shows the rest of the team what he has written: WE'RE FUCKED!

The voice on the other line finally pauses.

AGENT JOHNSON: OK, Jen. We'll see what we can do. We're going to do our best to make this happen. In the meantime, you're going to be alright? He's going to be alright?

Silence. The line goes dead.

The other officers rush toward Agent Johnson, who looks shell-shocked.

AGENT JOHNSON: I'm afraid it's not looking good, boys . . .

OFFICER LAURA HESS (forties) grunts behind Agent Johnson. She's been on the force for fifteen years, so you'd think she'd be used to the sexism, but she's not.

AGENT JOHNSON: Sorry, Hess. Bad habit.

Officer Hess doesn't reply.

AGENT JOHNSON (cont'd): Listen folks, no use in wasting any more time. Let's get out of here while we still can to catch some Z's.

MALE POLICE OFFICER: What are you talking about? She's got a hostage in there. We've got to try to negotiate. A man's in there . . .

He looks down at his notepad, searching for a name.

MALE POLICE OFFICER (cont'd): His name is Ryan. Looks like they're roommates?

AGENT JOHNSON: (sighs) Not roommates. He's the boyfriend.

MALE POLICE OFFICER: I don't get it. Why is she holding him? What does she want?

AGENT JOHNSON: It doesn't matter. He's a goner. We can't get to him. Or her. It's gonna be a shit show.

MALE POLICE OFFICER: (frustrated) What are you talking about? What the hell does she want that's so impossible to get?

AGENT JOHNSON: (angrily) Goddamnit. She wants to get married, you son of a bitch. Four years they've been together. What do you think she wants? It's not good. Not once, in thirty years of doing this, has this situation gotten resolved the way we want it to. Not once.

MALE POLICE OFFICER: Well, what does he say? This Ryan character.

AGENT JOHNSON: Get this, he says he never thought about it.

MALE POLICE OFFICER: Never thought about it? But it's been four years!

AGENT JOHNSON: Yah, well, tell him that.

OFFICER HESS: Well, something like that happened with my husband. We had been together for three years, and I basically told him to shit or get off the pot. I guess he shat.

Agent Johnson considers this.

AGENT JOHNSON: You're a lucky woman. Most guys don't take to threats that well. It sounds like you may just be the exception to the rule.

MALE POLICE OFFICER: (mouths) Is that a real thing?

The police officers stand down. Agent Johnson takes off his vest as he gives one last rueful glance at the building.

FADE OUT.

We shouldn't negotiate with terrorists, but what about our loved ones? Should you ever resort to an ultimatum?

My friend Sally is in her early thirties and happily married with a kid. When I ask her to tell me about the story of how her husband proposed, her face falls. *It took forever,* she laments, dwelling on the fact that they had been dating three years without him once hinting he was interested in marriage. Finally, Sally, who had her own property, a successful career, and pretty much had her life together in ways that I am still many light-years away from accomplishing, presented him with an eloquent ultimatum: *shit or get off the pot.* She knew what she wanted with her life, and if he didn't by now, she refused to wait any longer for him to figure it out. A few weeks later, he proposed—and the rest, as they say, is regularly documented on social media.

Sally advised me to do the same in my own relationship with Ryan, which had passed the three-year mark a few years ago. At the time, I wasn't crazy about the idea of forcing someone into lifelong commitment, but as the years continued to pass, and more friends got engaged, married, and had kids, I began to reconsider her advice. A few weeks before my thirty-third birthday, around the time Facebook alerted me that two more friends got engaged and a third was pregnant with her second child, I finally caved and told Ryan he had six months to propose or I was leaving. Here's the twist: *he didn't* propose . . . and a shocking double twist: *I didn't leave.*

Almost two years have passed since this all unfolded, but it's still painful to think about. For one, I looked like the biggest loser (and not the good weight-loss kind). Every well-meaning friend and expert suggested that the relationship was basically over, that I was foolishly holding onto a lost cause, and that I needed to stop thinking I was the *exception to the rule.* While on some level I trusted their advice, I wasn't ready to let go.

THE FIRST RULE OF ULTIMATUMS

Sally's story had me convinced that ultimatums were a sure thing. Any other outcome was *The Princess Bride*-level *inconceivable*, so when feelings of intense shame, self-doubt, and failure overcame me, America's No. 1 tough-love (borderline cruel) relationship talk radio host Dr. Laura was there to say *I told you so*. Just as in *Fight Club*, there is just one rule when it comes to ultimatums: *you must mean it*. She explains on her website, "The reason most ultimatums don't work is that the person making it is not ready to follow through. They hope and hope and hope the threat itself will be enough to make some magical change happen, but more often than not, it doesn't turn out that way . . ." In other words, do not issue an ultimatum unless your bags are already packed and you've booked an Airbnb for the next month. Without a viable plan B, you're likely to lose all credibility and leverage—both in your partner's eyes and your own.

Fun fact: Dr. Laura also calls marriage-related threats one of the "dumber ultimatums." "Who wants to get married to someone they have to threaten into marrying?" The most surefire way to have someone not do something is by trying to force them into it—this is why my cats no longer get baths. I already know this. I *knew* this, so why do I, and apparently loads of other dum-dums, still make these types of threats toward our loved ones?

One logical explanation points to the sunk cost fallacy, which we learned about in the last chapter. Couple this with the ticking time bomb we call our biological clocks, which demand a successful career, an Instagrammable home, a deliriously happy and sex-filled marriage, and 2.5 kids . . . all by the time we're in our mid-thirties, and it's no surprise that so many of us feel helpless, hopeless, and desperate enough to start making threats in an attempt to recuperate our losses.

One woman who was contemplating issuing a marriage ultimatum to her boyfriend of a year and a half posted on the wedding website, weddingbee.com, seeking the advice of other brides who had gone through with their own. A procession of brides (and future brides)—more than 155—provided a range of responses. A handful of women expressed regret at having waited so long, wishing they had issued the threat sooner, because it helped them realize that their partners were not *the one* after all. Others had zero regrets and were thrilled to get their hard-earned proposals. But some who extracted their proposals through intimidation tactics later admitted that their brute force might have sullied the sentiment and sincerity of the moment. Moreover, one woman who got engaged via ultimatum found herself experiencing déjà vu when her fiancé dragged his feet during the wedding planning, refusing to commit to either a date or a venue.

For these women, as well as myself, the ultimatums seemed to represent an unhealthy, fear-driven, last-ditch effort to prove to the world that we were, in fact, normal and totally loveable. I spoke to Jerry D. Smith, a psychologist and hostage negotiator, about this and he agreed, explaining that many resort to ultimatums as a form of self-defense. *I'll hurt them before they get a chance to hurt me.* And the more neglected we feel, the more inclined we are to turn to desperate measures. In some ways, it sounds like people who threaten their loved ones are guilty of committing emotional terrorism.

To find out if I was as evil as ISIS, I turned to David M. White, a law professor who trains with the NYPD Negotiation Team and assists the FBI in crisis negotiation. He patiently explained that not all crises are created equal. Only 4 percent of crisis situations are considered real hostage situations, where a perpetrator is willing to trade hostages for something else, such as cash, an escape route, or naked pictures of Bea Arthur. These types of crises are also favored by terrorist organizations and the producers of the *Taken* movie franchise. The vast majority of crisis situations (96 percent!) are not hostage situations, yet are considered far more dangerous. For example, a man who isn't asking for anything except to kill his family and himself because he is angry with his wife falls into this category. Because these showdowns are often sparked by personal and emotionally charged vendettas, the people who are taken against their will are not called hostages, but, rather ominously, victims or victims-to-be.

Negotiating hostages, for the most part, is effective in many cases, according to Smith. "Research indicates that most situations in which negotiations are informally or formally initiated are resolved without loss of life . . . because most people do not want to be in the situation, and they want the negotiation to help them find a way out." This resonates with my own experiences. I don't want to hurt anybody, least of all someone I love. In fact, conflict was the furthest thing from my mind when giving my own marriage ultimatum. Believe it or not, I thought I was doing my part to save the relationship.

On the bright side, the more I learn about real-life crisis situations, the less I see myself as a true terrorist, emotional or otherwise.

CRISIS NEGOTIATION 101

Despite the fact that he always finds a way to retrieve his kidnapped daughter or wife, Liam Neeson's character in *Taken* is not a gifted crisis negotiator. He would have been much better off and less injured had he employed the Behavioral Change Stairway Model, a five-step plan developed by the FBI to help get people to change their minds. If executed correctly, this method can (supposedly) mitigate any crisis situation, including the worst relationship quagmires. See an example below:

Behavioral Change Stairway Model

The threat: *If we don't get engaged in six months, our relationship is over.*

Step 1. Active Listening

> **Tactic:** This is hands-down the most important, most difficult, and most time-consuming of the steps, as it requires you to shut up and just listen to the other person. Crisis negotiators are, in fact, taught to "revel in silence" and offer only minimal feedback through emotional labeling. This tactic helps negotiators to gradually peel back the layers of the perpetrator's motivations and find out their true interests.

> **Try this . . .**

> Ryan: "Help me understand why you want to get married."

> Jen: "Everyone around me is getting married. I feel like a complete failure. In addition to the pressure I'm getting from my family, I feel like my window for having kids is closing very quickly. I would like to have kids while I still have the energy. And I would prefer not to have to change diapers for the kids and myself.

> Ryan: "Mmhmm. I see."

> Jen: *Lists additional reasons in an Oscar-worthy ninety-minute speech.*

> **Not that . . .**

> Ryan: "What's wrong with you? Why do you want to get married so badly?"

> Jen: "What's wrong with YOU, you asshole?

Step 2. Empathy

Tactic: The negotiator should relate a similar situation to show their understanding and validation of your feelings.

Try this . . .

Ryan: "I understand how stressful this pressure from your family and your biological clock to get married is. I feel it, too."

Not that . . .

Ryan: "I don't get why you're in such a rush. We have all the time in the world. In the grand scheme of things, this is not that important."

Step 3. Rapport

Tactic: Trust begins to form and a relationship begins to develop.

Try this . . .

Jen: "OK. I'm glad to hear that you are feeling this way, too."

Not that . . .

Jen: "FUUUUUCK YOUUUUUU."

Step 4. Influence

Tactic: Together, you can start to lay out the framework for a game plan, also called a "come out" plan. The negotiator should relate a similar situation to show their understanding and validation of your feelings.

Try this . . .

Ryan: "Well I would like to get married to you, and only you. But I'm not ready right now because of [fill in the blank (e.g., I don't feel financially ready, I'm only on season three of *Game of Thrones*, I'm being sued)]. I can promise you that there is no one else and there will never be anyone else. And I know I will be ready soon. Other than getting married right this second, tell me what I can do to make this relationship work for you."

Jen: "I am ready right now. And the only thing that will make me happy other than you proposing right this minute, is possibly doing it the next minute."

Ryan: "Come on."

Jen: "Just kidding. Not really. Um. It helps to know that you only want to be with me, but what would help more is if you promise to keep me informed of where you are at, and that you let me know as soon as you are ready."

Ryan: "Maybe we can look at engagement rings together this weekend, just so you know that I am serious about this."

Not that . . .

Ryan: "When you threaten me like this, it makes me want to marry you less."

Jen: "That makes two of us. I don't even know what I ever saw in you."

Ryan: "When did you become such a bitch?"

Jen: "Since you were an asshole, so since birth. I can't believe I thought we ever loved each other."

Ryan: "I don't get why you're in such a rush. We have all the time in the world. In the grand scheme of things, this is not that important . . ."

Jen: "If you say I'm in a rush one more time, I'm going to stab you."

Step 5. Behavioral Change

Tactic: If done correctly, both parties come to a mutually satisfying agreement or a plan, so that the perpetrator can put her gun down, so to speak, and exit negotiations.

Try this . . .

Jen: "Okay. I can just email you all the rings I like from my Pinterest board."

Ryan: "So do you want to stay with me?"

Jen: "I do."

Not that . . .

Jen: "Forget waiting six months. I'm leaving now."

Ryan: "Maybe that's a good idea."

Jen: "Have a nice life."

WHY YOU NO LONGER HAVE THE POWER

As kids, my brother and I used to reenact the opening scene from our favorite animated television show, *He-Man and the Masters of the Universe*, in which our hero slowly pulls out a sword from the sheath on his back and majestically points it toward the sky, as the three of us (my brother, me, and He-Man) in unison bellowed, "By the power of Grayskull . . . I have the power!" For those brief, glorious moments, I did have the *power*.

A similar feeling of unstoppable, intoxicating power washes over me during the outset of a new romantic relationship. Perhaps you are familiar with that deliciously satisfying, yet fleeting feeling that occurs when you are being pursued by someone who you actually want to be pursued by. He's blowing up your phone with calls or texts; you wait up to two, maybe even three days before responding. He's making romantic overtures taken straight out of '90s Boyz II Men music videos; you hum and haw about possibly squeezing him into your schedule next week. At which point it joyfully dawns on you: *I have the power!*

Once fully empowered, you can slowly let down your guard and open up the emotional fortress. Little by little, you return his calls a bit sooner. You begin to spend more time with him. You reciprocate his Boyz II Men tenderness with En Vogue enthusiasm. But all of a sudden, the spell has been broken. Like the Forever 21 jewelry that disintegrated in your hands as soon as you paid for it, so has your upper hand. The power dynamic has suddenly and inexplicably turned against you. Now it is you who is calling and texting him at all hours of the day, employing friends to carefully edit every text and emoji for quality assurance and low-to-moderate levels of desperation. You are the one trying to make plans for Friday night, only to receive an ambivalent text Sunday morning saying, "Sorry, I was busy."

This sudden shift in power begs the question, how can you be the object of one's affection one minute and the victim of a screened call the next? The answer, according to Dan Scotti, writer at *Elite Daily,* is the principle of least interest, which "pretty much grants the upper hand in any relationship to the one who gives the least amount of f*cks about it." In other words, the key to feeling empowered in a relationship is to care as little as possible about it.

First coined in 1937 by sociologist Willard Waller, the principle of least interest describes a situation where both partners are not equally invested in the relationship, and the person who is less interested or feels like he has less to lose has the most power and control. According to Rhonda R. Buckley, an associate professor of family sciences at Texas Woman's University, "there are a number of ways that a less interested partner can potentially exploit the deeper connection of a more invested partner," notably through economic or sexual manipulation. Case in point: one of my friends was so enamored by her unemployed and ambivalent, but *really talented*, artist boyfriend, that she paid for everything in their relationship for years before finally finding herself in a pit of debt and despair.

The principle of least interest does not discriminate against age, gender, or type of pairing. It is an equal opportunity relationship killer. The woman may rule the relationship during the courtship phase, only to be dethroned once the man feels like he has sufficiently captured her attention, and vice versa. And not that any of us need to hear this special message from Captain Obvious, but healthy relationships generally require equal(ish) investment and commitment from both partners.

YOU CAN'T FORCE SOMEONE TO FALL IN LOVE WITH YOU, OR CAN YOU?

There is a consensus in self-help land and popular psychology that you can't force someone to love you, despite the plethora of happy Internet testimonials from formerly brokenhearted men and women who credit Dr. Lukas, an alleged miracle-working spell caster in Nigeria, for returning their former loves to them.

There's also Leanne.

I have never met Leanne, but I know everything about her. She was the ex-girlfriend of Joe before he and I started dating. Their relationship did not end well. She had moved across the country to be with him, only to have him break up with her shortly afterward. Naturally, she was hurt and furious—I didn't blame her for that. But for everything she did afterward, I did.

Weeks into Joe's and my budding romance, the phone calls began. At first, I didn't think twice when he would disappear into a room for hours to talk to her. Breakups are painful, and sometimes the only thing that can get you through them is knowing that the other person still cares about you on some level. But soon the quality and quantity of the calls became so frequent and interminable that I wondered if he had taken a job as customer service rep for Comcast. His frequent disappearances began to affect our social life, too. He once left me stranded with another couple during a double date to take her call. When he finally returned an hour later, instead of an apology, he told me he had to leave. Before I could open my mouth in protest, he was gone. The other couple ended up taking me home. Sadly, my dignity wasn't able to make it home with me.

Joe was still on the phone with her when I returned home. I was fuming, but he barely acknowledged me. For a second I wondered if he was upset with me. Like I was the one who ruined his evening and embarrassed him in front of his friends. Oh wait, no, I was the sane one. When he finally hung up, a look of gravity came over his face as he said, "Leanne threatened to kill herself tonight."

The world stood still. I felt like an asshole. Yes, I had been humiliated and disappointed by the night's activities, but none of it was going to make me end my life. Stricken, I asked him what happened. "She's just having a really hard time right now . . . with everything," he responded without looking at me. I assumed I was part of the everything, and he did nothing to reassure me otherwise. From that point on, our relationship hinged precariously on her moods, which gradually became more desperate and manic. Joe ceased being my boyfriend (or hers even), and turned into Leanne's personal 911 emergency operator. He urged her to get professional help, but she always refused. As the weeks turned into months, it began to appear more like Leanne's threats of taking her own life were really a manipulative scheme to win Joe back. And it eventually worked.

One night Joe came clean and admitted that he had cheated on me with her. While he was apologetic, he still tried to shift any blame from himself to her condition: "You know how hard things have been for her. She just started kissing me, and I couldn't bear to hurt her after what she's been through." The crazy thing is that I believed him that first time. The second time he cheated on me, however, I didn't.

Shortly after we ended things, social media alerted me that Leanne and Joe were back together, and they have remained together since. As someone who can provide a direct eyewitness account of how their love story unfolded, I will admit that you can absolutely force someone into a relationship. But will it truly make either of you happy or emotionally satisfied?

Jessica Walsh and Timothy Goodman, two hip, attractive New York singles, turned their lives into a science experiment to answer this question. Inspired by the wisdom that it takes forty days to change a bad habit, the two friends decided to date each other for a month and change to see if they could fall in love. But first ground rules were established. They had to see each other every day, go on at least three dates per week, and visit a couple's therapist weekly. On one weird date they held hands the entire day, even during bathroom breaks. After their self-mandated courtship challenge was complete, the couple reported they had, in fact, developed genuine feelings for each other, but still ended up breaking things off on the last day. Timothy later admitted in an interview that toward the end of the experiment, he began to suspect their love connection was not quite fully formed. Jessica, on the other hand, had developed stronger feelings for him, but within three months post-challenge she was already seeing someone new. Even though their forced love caterpillar died in the cocoon, they both fluttered away with their fifteen minutes of fame, plus a sweet book deal.

Chapter 7
Love and . . . Marriage

Why marriage is so close, yet so far away.

If 2.1 million couples get married every year, *why aren't I married yet?* This is a question that I have heard time and time again, mostly because when I'm not wondering it aloud, a friend or family member is directly inquiring me to my face. No one is more disappointed than me when the answer is *I don't know.* As you have probably deduced, Ryan is not ready for marriage, whereas I am. Our mismatched timing has been an issue for the past several years, and in some ways our relationship has remained stunted because of it. Whenever I ask Ryan why he isn't ready or, more importantly, when he will be ready, the answer from him is usually *I don't know.*

For a long time, I interpreted this ambivalence as an attack against me and our relationship, a sign that I was neither lovable nor worthy of commitment—even though his regular proclamations of love and commitment suggested otherwise. To me (and everyone else but him) it seemed so moronically simple: If you love each other, you get married. *Right?* When I set out to write this chapter, I imagined that most of the research and experts I would talk to would support this rudimentary theory of romantic progression (as well as nursery rhymes)—first comes love, then comes marriage, then comes baby in the baby carriage—but in practice, this wasn't the case. What I ended up discovering was that when it comes to modern marriage, there is so much *I don't know.*

The first thing I didn't know? Ryan isn't the only one who harbors doubts about marriage.

MARRIAGE (RATES) HAVE BEEN GOING DOWNHILL FOR AWHILE

Ever since I attended my first wedding at the age of six (It was Ken and Barbie's; a tasteful and elegant summer affair on my Strawberry Shortcake bedspread, I gave the bride away, served as the officiant, and was the only guest in attendance), I assumed marriage was something that automatically happened to everyone. This was the late 1980s, the era in which marriage rates began seeing a steady decline in the US. Fast-forward to today where marriage rates are the lowest they've ever been. A 2012 Pew Research Center study found one in five adults ages twenty-five and older have never said their *I dos,* compared to one in ten adults in the same age range during 1960. But marriage doubts aren't limited to the US, according to Philip N. Cohen, a sociologist at the University of Maryland, who analyzed global demographic data and found that 87 percent of the world's population is currently living in countries where marriage rates have been plummeting since the 1980s.

If and when people do decide to tie the knot, they are waiting a lot longer to do so. Current data shows that the median ages at which men and women get married are twenty-nine and twenty-seven, five years older than the average age in the 1980s. So what gives?

WHOSE FAULT IS IT ANYWAY?

It turns out both women and men, as well as modern social mores, are responsible for these declining numbers. The feminist movement of the 1960s and '70s has been largely credited with shifting gender roles and perceptions, particularly in the realm of marriage. Women were empowered to find work outside of the home, pursue higher education, and exercise control over their bodies and birthing schedules, thanks in large part to the birth control pill. In fact, a Harvard research study found the pill to be a significant factor in a woman's decision to pursue long-term education and in marrying age. Higher education opened doors to higher-paying jobs and financial independence, so women no longer required or depended on husbands for their livelihood. This movement clearly heralded the discontinuation of the traditional gender paradigm where man is God and woman is his pregnant, yet dutiful, cleaning lady.

In recent years, the resistance and delay of marriage has also been blamed on the ease and accessibility of casual sex, which is now more tolerated than ever by society. Long gone are the days when people were waiting to have sex until marriage (unless you're a Duggar). Some people don't even wait to learn each other's names before pounding their private parts. Hookup apps like Tinder treat sex like a delivery service—where a stranger will do you in half an hour or less. For men at least, when sex is this easy to come by, there is little incentive to work . . . or walk down the aisle for it, according to a team of Rutgers University researchers that came to this conclusion after interviewing a group of sixty straight men between the ages of twenty-five and thirty-three.

But here's some promising news: just because people are postponing marriage, it doesn't mean it's never going to happen. The majority of us—86 percent of us, to be exact—will be married by our late forties, says Helen Fisher, a biological anthropologist and (probably) the world's foremost expert on love. She also tells me there is a third major reason why people today are so reluctant about marriage: divorce.

The D-word, she explains, is making millennials, especially, "absolutely terrified of marriage." With good reason—even though the myth of the 50 percent divorce rate has been mostly debunked (at its peak, researchers say the divorce rate was 41 percent in the early 1980s and has been steadily declining), it's difficult to ignore the potential havoc it can wreak on a family. Millennials are also the children of baby boomers, who are recognized as the most divorced generation in history, with a divorce rate that has doubled since the 1990s. In fact, several of my single friends who are the children of divorce admit their parents' split negatively influenced the way they view marriage. This is where "slow love" comes in. As Fisher described it, slow love is "an extension of the precommitment stage," or the relationship gray area where you find hookup culture, one-night stands, friends with benefits, and cohabitation (without marriage).

As the term suggests, slow love gives couples the opportunity to *try before they buy* into commitment. In other words, we should treat our mating prospects like samples at Costco. While this sounds reckless (and unequivocally unromantic), Fisher argues the opposite. For those who "want to know everything about the other person before they tie the knot," this caution affords them the ability to weed out the losers from the winners and preemptively shut down a bad coupling before things get too far.

While slow love sounds like a relatively new trend for the casual sex- and tech-obsessed generation, it's more like your mom's wardrobe, a retro fad making an overdue comeback.

"We are shedding 10,000 years of farming tradition, where a woman's place was in the home, man was head of the household, and marriage was 'til death do us part,'" Fisher explained to me. For more than a million years, the earliest humans lived in hunter-gatherer societies, where men and women both worked outside of the home and essentially earned a double income. This mutual interdependence ensured partnership and gender equality in every aspect of life, from the boardroom to the bedroom. Who knew cavemen were so evolved, *right?*

Fisher also told me that most modern men, in fact, embrace gender equality and feminism—at least when it comes to romance. "Men wish that women would take more initiative going for the first kiss, suggesting sex, asking for a phone number. Men want that. But women don't do that." Supporting her point is a 2013 Match.com survey in which 92 percent of guys said they would be comfortable being asked out by a gal. But she's right. *I don't do that.* And more importantly, *I don't want to do that.* The one and only time I made the first move was via AIM chat when I was a giddy sixteen-year-old confessing my I-like-you-more-than-a-friend feelings to my crush, Andrew. After hours of internal debate, I finally settled on the short and sweet, "I think you're cute." To which he replied as if I were applying for a position at his company, "FYI, thanks but I'm not interested." FYI, I still can't believe that he wrote FYI in a chat. And bonus FYI, I'm not alone in not being interested in asking men out. Despite all the myriad magazine articles and experts listing the buzzy benefits of equal-opportunity courtship, one 2011 online study finds 93 percent of women still prefer to be asked out, compared to just 16 percent of men. At the same time, I understand this is a fundamentally sexist and outdated courtship system. It originated in a time when a woman's value was determined by only three parts of her sum: an undisturbed hymen, culinary skills, and a knack for producing male heirs.

LOVE ≠ MARRIAGE

For the first marriages, which took place in Mesopotamia 4,000 years ago, it was business, not pleasure, that brought the happy couple together. These unions were legal contracts between a woman's father and her groom (or their families), "designed to assure and perpetuate an orderly society," according to historian Stephen Bertman. This devotion to practicality continued as marriage began to spread to other cultures. Getting hitched was all about mergers and acquisitions—making good business deals, securing heirs, or accumulating power. *But what about love?* "Though there was an inevitable emotional component to marriage," wrote Bertman in the *Handbook to Life in Ancient Mesopotamia,* "its prime intent in the eyes of the state was not companionship but procreation; not personal happiness in the present but communal continuity for the future." In fact, many cultures found marriage based on love to be foolish. In their book *The New I Do,* Susan Pease Gadoua and Vicki Larson write, "Indeed, love in marriage was seen as ludicrous, immoral, and even detrimental, as it posed a threat to other important relationships, such as the alliance with parents or a detraction from one's devotion to God."

That more than half of all global marriages are arranged marriages indicates many people still feel this way. And, over the years, there have been countless news articles and stories touting the benefits of an arranged pairing over one based purely on love. One of the most cited statistics is the lower divorce rate for an arranged union, which according to the website StatisticBrain.com, is 6.3 percent—significantly lower than the 40 percent(ish) divorce rate in the US. Although it is necessary to point out that also included in this tally are the 11 percent of girls in developing countries who are forced to get married by the time they're fifteen and for the most part are unable to legally seek out a divorce even if they wanted one.

The truth is romance only entered the marriage bed a few centuries ago. The seventeenth- and eighteenth-century philosophers of the Enlightenment period were the first to prioritize love and happiness, not wealth or power, as reasons to marry. Later, the Industrial Revolution of the nineteenth century helped build a burgeoning middle class, which meant people could now afford to take their love life into their own hands.

MONOGAMY ≠ MARRIAGE

Did you know only about 5 percent of the animal kingdom is monogamous? This loyal group of animals who believe in 'til death do us part includes prairie voles (which we'll talk about later), French angelfish, wolves, beavers, bald eagles, swans, and geese. In case you were wondering, this group does not include humans.

In fact, monogamy is antithetical to human nature, argues Christopher Ryan, an evolutionary psychologist who has extensively researched how physiology, archaeology, biology, and anthropology have influenced the sexual evolution. It turns out our hunter-gatherer ancestors (the same ones Helen Fisher referred to earlier) were never that interested in finding and settling down with their soul mate. Instead these early men and women practiced "fierce egalitarianism," or a communal environment where everything, including home, food, and sexual partners, was shared à la *Bachelor in Paradise*. However, this all changed with the advent of farming culture, which introduced the concepts of property and ownership. Suddenly what's mine was no longer yours, especially when sexual partners and offspring were concerned. In an interview with *Salon.com* Ryan explained, "When you have agriculture, men started to worry about whether or not certain children were theirs biologically, because they wanted to leave their accumulated property to their own child." So you see, monogamy was never about only having eyes for that special someone. Like arranged marriages, it was simply a pragmatic tool for property management and other business affairs.

In an *Alternet* article titled, "Why is monogamy idealized when most people aren't monogamous?" clinical psychologist David J. Ley also debunks the myth of monogamy in a similarly unromantic fashion. But first, let's address his claim that most people aren't monogamous. It sounds crazy to my puritan ears, too—but it's true! Throughout world history polygamy has been one of the most accepted and prevalent forms of marriage—and it still is. Today, it is believed that only 16 percent of world cultures enforce monogamy. If so few cultures are practicing monogamy, why is it still treated as the gold standard of relationships? In short, monogamy was considered the most beneficial for society. Ley wrote, "In polygyny [or polygamy] powerful men gather the most desirable women for themselves. And less powerful men 'go hungry,' wifeless . . . Those men who couldn't compete, didn't get to have even a single wife, and thus didn't have children. So what did those men do with their time? . . . It appears they got into lots of trouble."

He is referring to recent anthropological studies which found that monogamy has historically helped society stay safer. If men could have wives and children, they were less likely to engage in risky and criminal behaviors. And less crime meant more travel, innovation, and commerce—all signs of a thriving community. Even now, societies that allow men to take multiple wives have higher crime rates involving men. Still, Ley notes that just because some modern societies deem one wife is enough for one man, it hasn't stopped that one man (or wife) from pursuing multiple side pieces. Celebrities, politicians, and the 36 million users on AshleyMadison.com can all attest to that.

So is monogamy a sham in marriage? It depends. If you've been raised by heteronormative Disney ideals, like I have, then the answer is no, but the growing number of consensually non-monogamous relationships (CNM for short) over the past few years suggests otherwise. Based on one study of 9,000 singles, researchers surmise 20 percent of the dating population has engaged in a CNM relationship at least once. From open marriages to poly relationships, CNM setups are unique to each individual couple or group. Whether parties allow each other to partake in discreet Tinder hookups or hold regularly scheduled Sunday night *Game of Thrones* orgy reenactments must be decided and agreed upon by all affected parties. While CNM relationships are still largely stigmatized by mainstream America, at least one mainstream business is taking a different approach. OKCupid, which is considered one of the most open-minded dating platforms, was the first to create "nonmonogamous" and "open relationship" options for relationship status, as well as offer twelve sexual orientation and twenty-two gender options on its platform.

There are other clear signs—at least in pop culture—that suggest the CNM taboo is waning. Since 2016, the approval rating for polygamous marriages has been at 16 percent, which is double what it was in 2001. In fact, Americans are more accepting of polygamy than they are of cheating in monogamous marriages. This might be helped by humanizing portrayals of polygamous families cropping up in mainstream television, like HBO's drama *Big Love* and the TLC reality docu-series *Sister Wives*.

LOVE LIKE A PRAIRIE VOLE

Prairie voles are small rodents. They are officially part of the mouse family, but based on their Wikipedia picture look way more like cute hamsters. Male prairie voles are a lot like Tom Hanks; they are loyal nice guys who wants nothing more than to find their Rita Wilson vole and raise a family with her. (They're such hopeless romantics, they tend to fall madly in love with the first female they lose their virginity to!) However, their cousins, the male meadow voles, are nothing like them. They are considered the Leonardo DiCapri-voles of the vole family—promiscuous, lifelong bachelors whose sole objective is to burrow into the holes of as many lady voles as possible. Why are these two types of voles so different?

The answer lies in vasopressin, a hormone that is released during mating and linked to pair-bonding and monogamy. In prairie voles, the receptors for vaso-pressin are located in the area of the brain associated with pleasure, reward, and addiction, so each time Tom has sexy time with Rita, he feels closer and more bonded to her. Leonardo DiCapri-voles, on the other hand, house their vaso-pressin receptors somewhere in the brain's Siberia, an area absent of anything that resembles emotions.

To see if manipulating vasopressin levels would change the prairie voles' loyalty, scientists inhibited their vasopressin intake. And what do you know, Tom was suddenly less interested in spending time with Rita and didn't seem to care if other hunky voles were flirting with her. In other words, Tom was starting to act a lot like his cousin, Leo. Conversely, when Leonardo DiCapri-voles were directly injected with vasopressin in their brain's pleasure centers, they suddenly started to exhibit more pair-bonding behavior, like their cousin, Tom.

I know what you're thinking: Who cares about voles? Does this sorcery work on humans, too?

In 2008, a team of Swedish scientists decided to find out—minus the potentially illegal genetic testing. For the study, they recruited 550 pairs of adult twins who were all in long-term relationships. They found that 40 percent of the men tested carried allele 334, a gene that controls the production of vasopressin. When the partners of the twins were interviewed, the study's author, Hasse Walum, found, "women married to men who carry one or two copies of allele 334 were, on average, less satisfied with their relationship than women married to men who didn't carry this allele." In fact, men who carried two copies of the gene were twice as likely to have had a relationship crisis in the past year than those who had no copies. Of course, this doesn't mean that men who have one or more copies of this gene will definitely screw you over or make your relationship miserable . . . right? How convenient it would have been over the past decade to be able to purchase a home allele testing kit at the local pharmacy. It's a genius Kickstarter campaign, if you ask me.

When I think about my own relationships, I can't imagine them without monogamy. My relationship with Joe ultimately ended because of his serial cheating. But breaking up because of infidelity isn't necessarily the norm. Britain's *The Independent* newspaper reports, "somewhere between 20 percent to 65 percent of couples stay together after an affair."

THE RIGHT TIME FOR MARRIAGE

As an unmarried thirtysomething (who would very much like to be married) I have become something of an expert at Googling marriage statistics that make me feel both old and depressed. One of these data points comes from sociologist Nicholas Wolfinger, who upon analyzing a decade's worth of data from 10,000 national random test subjects, calculated the "perfect age" to get married: between twenty-eight and thirty-two. (Which is very close to the average marrying age for women and men in the US, twenty-seven and twenty-nine, respectively.)

Couples who get hitched during this four-year window are the least likely to get a divorce. "The odds of divorce decline as you age from your teenage years through your late twenties and early thirties," he explains. "Thereafter, the chances of divorce go up again as you move into your late thirties and early forties."

That couples who marry young tend to uncouple in greater numbers does not surprise Wolfinger, who jokes with me, "Think back to your high school boyfriend or girlfriend—imagine what it would be like to marry them and you'll see why the divorce rate is so high." I laugh and agree with him, pretending that

I actually had a boyfriend in high school and not a bunch of Jonathan Taylor Thomas Tiger Beat posters that I would make out with every night.

What was unexpected, however, was how high the divorce rates were for those in their mid to late thirties, as "traditionally, the older you got married the less likely you were to get divorced." Wolfinger first began to notice this trend shift around 2000. He's not sure what the catalyst was for this sudden rise in marital breakups for people in their thirties, but my guess is that it's somehow connected to *Divorce Court*, which premiered in 1999. Before then, no one ever saw real-life relationships disintegrate in front of a live television audience. Perhaps adults at home found this to be the one thing on television they could try at home.

If you're someone who has aged out of the prime marrying age, as I just have, these findings are about as appealing as discovering an ingrown hair on your bikini line. On the other hand, if you're in your early twenties, his findings are something to celebrate. *Congratulations!* You still have a handful of years before people start feeling sorry for you and asking you over Thanksgiving dinner why you have two cats but no husband.

Unlike reality show stars becoming president, marrying older isn't only a US phenomenon. Researchers at *Priceonomics* found that among the world's most populous countries—Germany (33.1), Brazil (30.8), and Japan (30.5)—all ranked higher than the US (27.9) in terms of average marrying ages. They also discovered a correlation between wealth and marrying age, pointing out that people from wealthy countries, on average, got married later than those in poorer countries. And again, it's difficult to ignore the fact that in some of these situations, young girls and women are forced into marriage.

SORRY, YOU'RE TOO POOR TO GET MARRIED

Every time I visit the ATM, I worry that instead of giving me cash, it will just print me a receipt of a sad face or flash the words "Nice try" on-screen. You could say I have a complicated relationship with money. I mean, I love money, I think we're perfect for each other, and we have so much fun together, but money, unfortunately, doesn't really feel the same way about me. He always claims to be lost or on his way, but he rarely shows up, and when he finally does get here, he comes up a lot shorter than I had hoped. But what I love most about money is that when you have a bunch of it, you can do a lot of cool things with it, like book a trip to space ($500K), poop on a solid gold toilet ($1.5 million), be appointed Secretary of Education ($200 million) . . . and, most importantly, throw yourself a decent wedding!

According to wedding website *The Knot,* the average cost of a wedding hovers around $32,000. To put this cost into perspective, the US Census Bureau determines the median income for an American household is just over $53,000, which means some couples end up spending more than half of their yearly income on one day, or rather, a few exorbitantly expensive hours. This means that very few of us can afford to have the wedding of our dreams—or even the wedding of our budget nightmares, according to one survey that finds half of Americans have less than $1,000 in their savings accounts. Moreover, a wedding is just the first of many significant expenses to share with your life partner. In 2014, the median cost of a home in the US was $188,900—which can get you a cozy one-room cardboard box on a shady tree-lined street in San Francisco. And if you plan to have children, each one will cost you $233,610 (payments are spread out over eighteen years), according to a CNN report.

All of this brings us yet another important reason Americans aren't getting hitched like they used to. In fact, nearly a third of Americans don't feel financially ready to get married—the second most common reason for holding off marriage behind not finding the right person, according to a Pew study. While we all know (or have Internet stalked) those couples who are blessed with lots of capital—whether it be raised by their own work ethic or that of their parents—most of us cannot think about celebrating the happiest day of our lives without experiencing some pecuniary dread. In one recent study of 300 working- and middle-class people, researchers found the ever-expanding wage gap has slowly turned marriage into a luxury commodity, available only to the upper classes. According to Sarah Corse, the study's co-author, "Working-class people with insecure work and few resources, little stability, and no ability to plan for a foreseeable future become concerned with their own survival and often become unable to imagine being able to provide materially and emotionally for others."

Though I wouldn't classify myself as part of the working class, I, too, am mired in *too-depressing-to-calculate-because-my-brain-will-surely-explode* student loan debt, which routinely robs me of one-third of my monthly paycheck. The truth I'm realizing now is that even if Ryan was ready to propose, we might not be ready for the wedding and everything else that comes after.

ROOMMATES IN SIN

Even though Ryan and I are not married, we are cohabitating, which is nicer than saying "living in sin," which is how my mom likes to put it. When we moved in together six years ago, I had already created my wedding Pinterest board and decided on a nautical theme for the reception. Never in my wildest dreams did I think we would still only be roommates years later, but here we are. And we are hardly alone. A 2013 report from the National Center for Health Statistics reveals more couples than ever before are living together before marriage, with 48 percent of all straight women between the ages of fifteen and forty-four having lived with a partner they weren't married to, compared to just 34 percent in 1995. For many people, including Ryan and me, our decision to live together made sense financially, especially since we had just moved to one of the most expensive cities in the world. (We once accidentally bought a single crown of broccoli for $7.)

Over the years, I began to wonder if living in sin was somehow responsible for Ryan's reluctance to take the next step. Was that awful saying true? *Why would he buy the cow when he was getting my milk for free?* Not necessarily, according to the same National Center for Health Statistics research. Although the study found that couples were living together longer before marriage, jumping from thirteen months in 1995 to twenty-two months in 2006–2010, 40 percent of cohabitants still got married within three years. However, 32 percent did not get married but stayed together, while 27 percent broke up.

As much as I would like for Ryan and me to be more than roommates, there are still benefits to our current living arrangement. In addition to having someone to share meals with and reach the top shelf in the cupboard, one 2012 study finds some cohabitating couples are happier and healthier than their married counterparts. Researchers suggest it may have something to do with the couple having more freedom and space to themselves. Still, living together is not the same as marriage. And seven years into this relationship, simply cohabitating no longer feels like enough.

Chapter 8
Love and . . . Magic

Why we believe Miss Cleo knows more about our future than we do.

Every month, seventeen million people make a pilgrimage to Susan Miller's AstrologyZone.com, an eerily accurate Ouija board for the Internet. For more than twenty years, her famously lengthy horoscopes—accessible via web and app—have yielded legions of fans eager to learn what the planets have in store for them that month. *Don't sign contracts when Mercury is in retrograde. A new moon often heralds an auspicious, new beginning. Having Jupiter in your sign may signal upcoming world travel, so pack your bags!*

As both a regular visitor of the site and someone who has always been fascinated with the idea of astrology, fortune-telling, spells, and magic, I can't deny the inexplicable allure of inviting third-party mysticism into my personal life. There's something bizarre, yet freeing about being told that every single thing that has gone wrong with my life isn't my fault, but rather the fault of a faraway planet in retrograde. I mean, *what does retrograde even mean?*

That I haven't skipped a Susan Miller monthly forecast in more than half a decade should tell you something. But it's not just Susan I'm consulting for my existential life crises. I've shelled out hundreds of dollars for multiple in-person visits, Skype sessions, and phone chats with various fortune-tellers, healers, and practitioners of the occult. *But do I really believe in all this stuff?*

A TRIP TO THE MALL OF FORTUNE

My friend Lisa and I met the Nameless Vietnamese Fortune-Teller at the fittingly named Mall of Fortune, a rundown, yet bustling shopping center in the heart of Little Saigon in Orange County, California. This diminutive woman with no name also spoke no word of English, but was praised as an extremely gifted clairvoyant by Lisa's friend's sister's mechanic's aunt's second cousin's son's preschool playmate's great-great-grandfather's pool guy's pastor's cobbler's DirecTV salesman's cousin, who had received a scary-accurate reading about her boyfriend getting out of jail, which promptly came true!

Lisa and I considered ourselves to be healthy skeptics, but w*ho accurately predicts something like that?* We needed to see the nameless octogenarian for ourselves and determine whether she was legit. When we arrived, she was sitting with her hands primly folded at a table in the middle of a badly lit food court, an array of playing cards spread out in front of her. Another friend, Mimi, came with us to serve as our translator. No one was interested in small talk or pleasantries, so Lisa and I just plopped our $20 bills on the table in exchange for a sneak peek into our destiny.

Lisa went first. NVFT took her hand and stared at it blankly, as if she wasn't quite sure what she was looking at. As soon as she seemed to recognize what it was, she dropped it, somewhat irritated. She then proceeded to shuffle the deck in front of her, like a Vegas blackjack dealer, and randomly selected a card, a ten of hearts. She grimaced, seemingly unsatisfied, then returned it to the deck, before selecting a few others she seemed to like better. Mind you, this was a deck of regular playing cards, not tarot cards. Whether she was playing solitaire or reading a fortune was unclear at that point. Then, she turned to Mimi and spoke to her in hushed Vietnamese for what felt like five straight minutes. Since there weren't any hand gestures or even one English-sounding word, all we could do was hope that NVFT's permanent stink face did not portend a completely bleak future. When she finally finished dictating her prophecy, Mimi nodded at her and turned to us, "She says you're a hard worker. You're very good at your job."

Lisa and I eyed each other quizzically. *That's it?* We were both wondering how much Vietnamese Mimi truly understood. When it became clear that that was all she was getting, Lisa nodded and agreed. She really was a hard worker and very good at her job. But this wasn't enough, and certainly not worth $20. Lisa wanted more, specifically answers about her love life.

Mimi returned to NVFT and possibly relayed our concerns in what we were pretty sure was Vietnamese. NVFT seemed to comprehend and began to ramble on again for another few minutes before Mimi turned to us again: "She says that you have one more chance at love."

Lisa's eyes bulged. "What?" she exclaimed, breathlessly. Lisa, who at the time was dating a guy who was equal parts scumbag and charmer, was not pleased by the prediction. NVFT shook her head at Lisa and garbled something ominous, while wagging a finger at her.

Mimi continued, "Yeah, she says that if you don't find love this year, that's it. You won't have another shot. Sorry."

NVFT did not look sorry though. She looked bored. Lisa looked like she was going to cry. I wasn't sure what was worse for her, ending up with the charming scumbag or being alone *forever*. At this point, I was ready to forfeit my cash. I didn't need to pay someone to make me feel hopeless. I could do that all on my own, for free!

But NVFT honed in on me, taking my hands and observing my palms before casually tossing them back on the table. This time, she didn't even bother to consult the cards, which confirmed my earlier suspicion that our arrival had interrupted her card game. A look of consternation fell on her face, as she informed Mimi of what seemed to be yet another grave prognosis.

This time, Mimi had an expression of relief. She told me: "You are a daddy's girl. You have a great relationship with him." Neither of these things were remotely true.

"OK," I said wearily. Since she had already started, I figured *what the hell?* I asked Mimi to get some intel about my current relationship. What was going to happen to it? I was dating someone I was head over heels for. I mean, I was picking out wedding songs, and we had only been together for a few months.

After a short consultation, Mimi said, "Well, she doesn't know. She says maybe it'll work out, but it's up to you. You have the power in the relationship to go where you want to take it."

I didn't know exactly what to make of this. It didn't sound bad, but it didn't sound great either. Lisa was glaring at me. We both knew it was better than being subjected to her lifetime of "Table for one?" Before I knew it, the session was over and we found ourselves leaving the Mall of Fortune, less fortunate than when we had arrived.

So, did these predictions come true? Not at all.

Lisa and her hot scumbag inevitably ended things a few months later. At first, she resigned herself to being alone and even got a cat, but within a couple years, met and later married the love of her life, who was all parts perfect for her.

For myself, it turned out that I didn't have the power after all. The guy I was seeing cited a cross-country move that was scheduled for "sometime in the near future" as a reason to cut our relationship short. Nor did my relationship with my dad improve.

Even though our visit to NVFT took place almost a decade ago, Lisa and I still reminisce about our respective, alternative-fact-filled fortunes. Since then,

Lisa has retained her healthy skepticism of the metaphysical, while I have gotten only more curious. And I'm not sure why. You'd think I would have viewed these fallacies as a sign from the universe guiding me toward not relying on the universe for guidance, but I can't help it. I'm like Agent Mulder from *The X-Files*—I want to believe.

A BRIEF HISTORY OF ASTROLOGY, WHICH IS NOT MAGIC

When I talked to Susan Miller on the phone for this chapter, she made it adamantly clear that astrology is in no way shape or form *magic*. "I'm doing geometry all day long," she says. "Astrology is math." And, no matter what most of the scientific community argues, it really is. Astrology and its oft-confused counterpart, astronomy (which scientists consider the first "real" science), share the same origins, kind of like fraternal twins.

The first people to pay attention to what was happening in the sky were the ancient Babylonians. Around 1600 BC, they were so captivated by the position and movement of the stars and planets and their effect on nature that they came to worship them as gods. The Greeks and Romans agreed and gave these planet-gods the names they have now: Venus, Jupiter, Mars, and the rest of the space gang.

But over time, the love affair between astrology and science began to wane. The first signs of trouble emerged during the sixteenth century, when scientists began to differentiate between natural and judicial astrology. Natural astrology focused on how the celestial bodies influenced the elements, like the weather or ocean tides, whereas judicial astrology was concerned with how they might impact or predict human behavior. And like a WWE Royal Rumble, other parties also joined the fight—namely Christian thugs from the Reformation mafia, who didn't like the idea of astrology taking over God's religious turf. By the end of the century, astrology was condemned by the Church as well as some governments, and those who openly practiced astrology could be prosecuted and punished for witchcraft.

Although academic astrology still survived into the next century, medical advancement and scientific breakthroughs of the period further widened the chasm between the empirical and the divine. With both the Church and the scientific community now discrediting astrology, it was starting to look a lot more like GeoCities than Google.

Throughout the centuries, however, astrology has enjoyed noteworthy periods of revival. One of its most ostensibly legitimate comebacks occurred in the early twentieth century and was led by famed Swiss psychiatrist Carl Jung. His theory of synchronicity is basically the Grey Poupon to astrology's no-name mustard. Synchronicity explained meaningful coincidences and proved that everything in the universe was interconnected. For example, when you're thinking about a friend and she calls you seconds later. It's not a coinkydink, it's synchronicity! In addition to astrology, synchronicity has been compared to the law of attraction and the power of flow.

During the 1970s, which ushered in the New Age era of personal transformation and healing, astrology had another spiritual awakening, but this time, it completely dropped the science and focused solely on enlightenment and metaphysical aspects.

Of course, there are still plenty of those like Miller (and her army of followers) who remain devout believers in the science of astronomy. Jackie Slevin, an astrologer and the education director at the National Council for Geocosmic Research, is herself a true believer and teacher of all things Geocosmic. The council, she told me, boasts more than 1,500 members and is "considered the premier program for astrological education worldwide." On the scientific community's reluctance to accept astrology as a science, she admits, "It is very difficult to quantify astrology in terms of statistical analysis and come out with definitive conclusions, which is what they want and demand for validity." But she argues there is undeniable evidence that there's method in the moon's madness. During an eclipse, birds will fly outside of their given path and flowers will bloom at odd hours of the night, she explains. The tides, science has confirmed, are also controlled by the gravitational pull of the moon. Our bodies are made up of 75 percent water. The moon controls so much of nature, she says. "Aren't we nature, too?"

IN GOD WE TRUST?

Science writer and my former editor at *Psychology Today* Matt Hutson traces our belief in magic to our ancestors' germaphobia. Though they couldn't see or comprehend them, the earliest humans still instinctively knew that these invisible microorganisms could mess with their survival. Through time humans began to develop similar associations for other objects and esoteric concepts. But once medicine and technology became more advanced, as we learned in the history of astrology, things that were once inexplicable could now be explained by science.

Well, *almost everything.* Science is excellent at figuring out what is wrong with our bodies, but not with our hearts. No science experiment can solve the mystery of why I'm not married (yet), help me decide whether I should quit my job, or tell me at what age I will have a child. Which is likely why romance, career, and health are the top three topics of interest for the 15 percent of Americans who have sought some form of celestial or spiritual guidance. Today, psychic services make up a $2 billion industry, and it has seen a steady 2.4 percent annual growth since 2011. Sociologist Nicholas Wolfinger suspects this rise coincides with the gradual decline of organized religion over the past several decades. A 2015 Gallup poll finds only 42 percent of Americans have confidence in organized religion (*this is me*), compared to 68 percent in the 1970s. One splashy *Newsweek* headline even declared the general public trusts the police more than they do the church. This dovetails with findings from a 2014 Pew Research Center study, which indicate that Americans, millennials in particular, are less likely to identify as part of a religious group than they were nearly a decade before. This has me wondering: Has God jumped the shark?

For Marlene Vargas, co-owner of the House of Intuition, a successful metaphysical shop in Los Angeles, her own departure from religion is what inspired her to open up her store. Vargas was raised in a strict Catholic family, where even curiosity about the occult was forbidden. But a visit from the spirit of her recently deceased aunt changed everything, an event Vargas refers to as an "awakening." From that point forward, Vargas could no longer see the church or the priest as the only guides toward spiritual enlightenment. "I still believe in God, Jesus, and Buddha," she says. "I know they're all one. We all pray to the same source; they just have different names." In the end, it was a tarot reader, not God, Jesus, or Buddha, who instilled in her the courage and confidence to start her business, even though she was near bankruptcy. This was in 2010. Less than a decade later, she has expanded to two new locations and partnered with Urban Outfitters to sell a line of branded aura-cleansing, apothecary products.

Like Vargas, I am an avid practitioner of kitchen-sink spirituality. Growing up, I dreaded going to church. In my teenage service were some of the most terrifyingly condescending girls I have ever encountered. At church, I usually sat alone, surrounded by empty seats, which a pastor once declared to me "were filled with devils." Why he would say this to a child, or why devils would choose to come to church, I will never know. But it didn't matter—as soon as I heard the last "Amen," I was out the door. As far as I could tell, this was not the quality time with God that had been advertised.

Of course, some people, like my mom, do find community and comfort at church. Unlike me, she still goes to church and sits with friends, not demons.

After my father passed away, she found solace in the church, and even more so in God. Seeking a higher power in times of hardship is not unusual. In 2015, a team of international researchers from the University of Auckland and North Carolina State University analyzed the geography, religion, and agriculture data of more than a thousand societies and found belief in God was an effective coping mechanism even for early humans.

With astrology, tarot, and otherworldly spiritual guides, we no longer have to rely solely on God to make sense of the chaos that interrupts our lives. (And no offense to the guy upstairs, but God isn't as responsive as these other mediums, right?) After the assassination attempt on President Reagan, First Lady Nancy Reagan turned to astrologer Joan Quigley for guidance. For seven years, the astrologer had unprecedented access to White House affairs, allegedly influencing everything from timing press conferences to scheduling trips abroad. Talk shows regularly welcome psychics and mediums who can channel dead spirits in front of a live studio audience. And newer shows, like *Hollywood Medium* and *Long Island Medium*, star telegenic clairvoyants who offer necromancy on demand, proving that not even the afterlife is safe from reality TV. Oftentimes, these shows will exploit the "P.T. Barnum effect," named after the circus founder's famous adage, "There's a sucker born every minute." Readings or horoscopes that are ambiguous or vague enough so that something applies to you are a good example of this effect. Here's an example: *You love to go out with your friends and listen to music, but sometimes you like to stay home and go to bed early. You love to be happy. You hate to be sad. When you're hungry, you like to eat.* Does this sound like you? Or on TV, when you see a medium ask the hundreds of people in the studio audience if anyone knows someone with the letter M in their name. Still, even if it's all bogus, unlike organized religion, the church of the occult provides instant closure, catharsis, and hope—all for a nominal fee.

"It also provides meaning and order in an otherwise random universe," wrote Benjamin Radford in *Live Science*, in reference to Jung's theory of synchronicity, but can be applied to all forms of magical thinking. He cites a story about one of Jung's patients, who told him that when both her mother and grandmother died, a flock of birds gathered at her window. Her husband, who had symptoms of a heart problem, went to visit the doctor, and unbeknownst to her, collapsed on his way back home. While this was happening, she saw a flock of birds at her window—which she naturally assumed was a sign of his imminent death. It's a crazy coincidence, right?

Radford doesn't think so. "If you truly believe that the presence of birds is a portent of death, there are many questions that need to be examined: How many birds are needed? One? Dozens? Hundreds? Is it any type of bird? How soon before a person's death do they appear? . . . And even if the proposed synchronicity was true, how do we know whose death the birds' presence foretells?" That is to say, this *crazy coincidence* is really a cognitive behavior known as confirmation bias. Each time we assign more weight to evidence that confirms our beliefs or ignore or undervalue evidence that doesn't support our beliefs, we are guilty of confirmation bias. As you can imagine, this bias is a powerful tool for magical thinkers.

Confirmation bias is so powerful, it can even make believers out of nonbelievers, according to psychology professor and author Stuart Vyse. In his book, *Believing in Magic*, he details a psychology study that involved twelve astrology devotees and fourteen astrology skeptics. All participants were tasked with interviewing a person and finding out if the horoscope that had been written for him by a professional astrologer was accurate. The horoscope described the person as very outgoing. During the interviews, both the skeptics and the devotees spent most of their time asking questions that would confirm the person had outgoing behavior, such as "Do you like to go to parties?" instead of asking ones that might result in denial. The interviewee, by the way, was a plant of the experiment and was instructed to answer "yes" to every question, regardless of what they were, so any information the interviewers learned were based entirely on their own questions. So, what happened? Unsurprisingly, the devotees generally agreed that the horoscope was accurate. As believers, they were already primed to believe the horoscope, and the information from the interviews simply confirmed what they wanted to believe, clearly demonstrating confirmation bias. On the other hand, the skeptics, who asked more disconfirming questions, got more disconfirming responses and were less likely to agree with the horoscope, still proving the confirmation bias.

In 2006, confirmation bias was repackaged as *The Secret,* and thanks to Oprah's blessing, quickly became a bestselling self-help book and film. The secret (which wasn't a secret at all) effectively harnessed the power of the law of attraction—the belief that positive thinking generates positive results. When the book came out, I was in my early twenties and was immediately hooked. I listened to the audiobook almost every night and made a vision board, which was really just an ugly poster board collage covered in pictures of skinny women in bikinis, photos of Ryan Gosling, an Academy Award, and other things I wanted to "manifest" into my life at the time but never did. Manifesting is similar to ordering on Amazon. You put whatever your heart desires (e.g., a better job, *Hamilton* tickets, your boyfriend to propose) into your brain's shopping cart, then at checkout you simply tell the universe, "I am grateful for [whatever is in your cart]"—no credit card required. *That's it!* The trick is you must pretend that you already have whatever it is you want. The universe will be so touched (or confused) by your gratitude, that it will deliver your request, with free shipping!

There's just one catch. If for some reason your package doesn't get delivered, then it's all your fault. You did something wrong. The universe's customer service team will tell you that you weren't pretending hard enough or your gratitude wasn't authentic. This is because the only rule of the law of attraction is that "like attracts like," so everything good that happens is a result of your positivity, and everything bad, on some level, is caused by your own negativity. Obviously, there are some concerns with this formula. The big one that comes to mind is the Holocaust. *Did six million Jews really will the most horrific tragedy in history into existence through their negative thoughts?*

Perhaps it was not having a good answer to questions like the one above, or the fact that very few people were getting the goods they ordered, but over the past decade, *The Secret* and its practitioners have been mired in controversy and criticism, losing much of their juiciness and following.

WHEN YOU DON'T HAVE ANY CONTROL

While confirmation bias might convince us that the universe is an eager-to-please personal assistant that's at our beck and call, not everyone sees it that way. Some magical thinkers, like writer Rachel Hosie, view the universe primarily as an all-too-convenient scapegoat. In a piece for the UK's *The Independent* newspaper, she writes, "astrology gives people an excuse for their less than positive traits or actions." For example, someone might say, "It's not my fault I'm bad at decision-making, it's just because I'm a Libra."

This is true. On more than one occasion, I have blamed my stubbornness and need for attention on being a Leo. *It's who I am! Gotta love me!*

In psychology, the extent to which we believe we have power over our lives is called the locus of control. People who have an internal locus of control believe they affect and influence events and outcomes in their lives, whereas those who have an external locus feel powerless over what happens to them—it's all up to chance, fate, or other outside forces. Here's another way to think of it: imagine the internal locus being in the driver's seat, while the external locus is bound and gagged in the trunk of the car. According to behaviorist and author Robin H-C, the type of locus you have is defined by your upbringing. For example, kids who experience extreme stress, neglect, and abuse are more vulnerable to feeling helpless and powerless as adults.

A number of studies have also found that women are more likely than men to have an external locus of control. It's not difficult to see why. In general, women are socialized to be docile, conforming, and passive, as opposed to men, who are taught to be fearless, active, and tough. And when it comes to romance, men are taught to be the pursuer, and women their patient prey. Since the dawn of the farming revolution, women have lived at the whim of men, being traded and treated as little more than chattel or nonunionized baby factories.

Even though today's women have come a long way since then, we are still not as empowered or confident as, say, a mediocre white man. It was only less than a century ago that women successfully fought for the right to vote in the US. Meanwhile, across the world in Nepal, girls and women are still regularly exiled from their homes and forbidden from going to school or taking baths when they are menstruating, a superstitious practice called Chhaupadi. If the hallmarks of a strong internal locus of control are self-esteem and independence, which researchers say it is, then you can see why women aren't necessarily born with it. This might also explain why twice as many women than men have consulted a fortune-teller or psychic, according to a Pew Research Center study, and nearly every tarot reader I have talked to says the overwhelming majority of their clients are women or that the No. 1 most discussed subject is their romantic lives. Only Susan Miller disagreed with this assessment, informing me that nearly half of her website visitors are men.

Astrologer Jackie Slevin offers another perspective. Though she acknowledges astrology's association to an external locus, her job, after all, is to give insight about seemingly unavoidable circumstances, she believes the more you integrate astrology into your life, the more likely your locus will shift toward the internal. She explained to me, "The internal locus stems from confidence and knowledge of strengths and weaknesses, and astrology can pinpoint those strengths and weaknesses in their horoscopes. The more you know, the more you can meet the obstacles and surmount them."

HOW IMPORTANT IS ACCURACY?

Of the half dozen or so other-wordly spiritual guides I have consulted with since NVFT, I can honestly say that not one of these readings was all that accurate about my past, present, or, most importantly, my future. Even Susan Miller's sacred monthly forecasts don't quite provide the assurances that I desire. My friend Lily, who has also met with her share of spiritual healers, astrologers, and tarot readers for guidance in her love life, admits their accuracy rate is generally not great either. But she continues to seek their counsel because they offer something more powerful than plain facts: hope. Hope that she will find the man she's going to marry, which becomes more promising when her Sun in Taurus is receiving positive aspects from an outer planet.

"Astrology is not predestination," says Miller, when I ask her what she tells people who complain when their predictions don't come true. "I see an opportunity, but you have to make an action." If someone complains about not meeting someone, even though it is written in their chart, she'll ask, "Did you go out? Did you do anything different?" In other words, astrology is not a Ronco Rotisserie. You can't just set it and forget it.

Erin K. Smith gives mobile tarot readings out of a converted and ultra-Instagrammable food truck. My friend Jasmine met Erin at Coachella in 2016 and was immediately drawn to her energy, so when I wanted to get some guidance about this book and whether it would doom my relationship with Ryan, I gave her a call. Because of the distance, we decided on a one-hour Skype session, where one of the first things she tells me is "No future is written in stone." Her job, she insists, is not to be a psychic, but to offer wisdom and greater personal insight by tapping into her intuitive abilities, a set of skills which she believes everyone has. To her, tarot is "a visual map to investigate what is going on below the level of consciousness in a person." Because we operate our lives primarily at the surface, we are largely unaware of how powerful the subconscious is in guiding or blocking our decisions. One client called one of her tarot sessions as valuable as six months of therapy.

Dubbed the "unofficial commissioner of public spirit of NYC" by *The New Yorker,* Mama Donna has been organizing and leading large-scale spiritual and ritualistic ceremonies for the public in the city for forty-two years. On her colorful resume, you'll also find: urban shaman, spiritual teacher, award-winning author, tarot reader, and ritual consultant for the television and film industry. And in each of these mediums, she channels just one important message: empowerment. Like Smith, she believes tarot sessions are a way to "connect to your inner wisdom" and find "affirmation and confirmation in what you already feel."

If magical thinking provides hope, opportunity, affirmation, and empowerment for the future, is it really such a bad thing to buy into it?

PRACTICAL MAGIC: THE SCIENCE OF GUT FEELINGS

Jasmine is blessed with an extraordinary gift: her "vibes." As long as I've known her, she's employed her vibes to steer us away from bad decisions, like hooking up with the wrong guy or trying to hook up with him again when we think she's not looking. She is like an eerily accurate human Magic 8 Ball. Luckily, Jasmine generously offers her services pro bono—or is willing to barter her clairvoyance for cocktails, which comes in handy when you've spent all your money on lottery tickets.

Believe it or not, Jasmine's eerily accurate vibes are biologically based on the only true form of scientifically proven magic in existence. We just call them something else: gut feelings.

Neuroscientist Louann Brizendine describes gut feelings as part of "our protections, alerts, and alarms"—and for women, at least, are generally quite reliable. In her book, *The Female Brain*, she writes, "[O]verall, the female brain is gifted at quickly assessing the thoughts, beliefs and intentions of others, based on the smallest hints . . . [M]en don't seem to have the same innate ability to read faces and tone of voice for emotional nuance." Even during childhood, girls are far more advanced than boys in their ability "not only to observe, but also to imitate or mirror the hand gestures, body postures, breathing rates, gazes, and facial expressions of other people as a way of intuiting what they are feeling." (This could also explain why women are so good at charades!)

This cool psychic ability likely evolved from our female ancestors, who had to be on constant high alert in assessing their surroundings in order to protect their infants and themselves from outside dangers. In other words, next time you feel that something is off—whether it is in the pit of your stomach or a little voice in the back of your head—it probably is. And you don't even need Jasmine there to confirm it.

Chapter 9
Love and . . . The Girl Code

Why our friendships can suck just as much as our romantic relationships.

Chicks before Dicks. Sisters before Misters. Venus before Penis. Insert your own quippy tagline professing the importance of putting your girls above all else. In practice, however, our platonic female friendships are not always so easy breezy and can often be as equally complicated as our romantic relationships.

THE RULES OF THE GIRL CODE

We've all heard of the Bro Code—a widely recognized set of rules designed to preserve and protect male masculinity, most notably through strict adherence to the cardinal rule: *Bros before hoes.* But what is the Girl Code? Like the Bro Code, the Girl Code comes with its own catchy rhyming prepositional phrases, prioritizing friendship over romance, but as it turns out, this is only one minuscule section in the official Girl Code handbook.

Not too long ago, a group of four girlfriends and I, all in our mid-twenties to early thirties and with diverse cultural backgrounds, spent the evening discussing these rules. None of us had ever talked explicitly about the Girl Code before. It had always been "unwritten" or something we "just *know* to do." But because they are my good friends and knew I was nearing this book's deadline, they graciously agreed to help. Together, we compiled a list of ten important rules of the Girl Code, from what we guessed to be thousands, maybe even millions.

DISCLAIMER: I just want all of us to be clear that not every (or any) rule automatically applies to every group of friends. There may be some that you have never heard of or find completely absurd, but it doesn't mean they don't exist. Maybe you just have better friends than I do.

1. Thou shalt not hook up with or date someone a friend has ever had a crush on, dated, or expressed any interest in as a potential romantic partner.

2. Thou shalt not look at a friend's significant other in any manner that is even remotely suggestive of flirtation, sexuality, or excessive enthusiasm. Plainly speaking, treat friend's significant other "like they have no genitalia."

3. Thou shalt hate the same people that your friend hates. If you don't, you may not defend them or "give them the benefit of the doubt" when said friend is talking shit about them.

4. Thou shalt provide each friend a minimum of 1,000 hours of phone calls, Skype calls, text messages, or in-person therapy sessions during times of heartbreak or duress—all unpaid.

5. Thou shalt never purchase or wear the same outfit, makeup, or jewelry without explicit consent, either written or verbal, from originating friend.

6. Thou shalt not look more attractive than a friend if it's their special occasion, such as a wedding or a birthday. (One friend tells us, "My own sister wouldn't let any of her bridesmaids get their hair done for her wedding, incredulously asking them, 'Why would you get your hair done? It's my wedding!'")

7. Thou shalt not tell a friend that a guy is not that into her, doubly so if this is the truth.

8. Thou shalt always be on alert to swiftly rescue a friend from unwelcome male advances or attention (so friend does not look like a bitch).

9. Thou shalt avoid talking shit about a friend's significant other, even if said significant other is truly *the scum of the earth*.

10. Thou shalt not ditch or cancel plans with a friend for significant other without at least 24-hours' notice.

As every rule-breaker knows, the punishments for not following these ten commandments are swift and severe. One friend, Krista, learned this lesson in middle school during a life-changing game of Spin the Bottle. On her turn, the bottle pointed to a boy who was the crush of one of her girlfriends. As chaste as it was, their kiss signified the kiss of death for her friendship. The other girl accused Krista of betraying her and phone-treed the rest of the middle school girls to exile her. With her apologies and attempts at reconciliation ignored, Krista spent weeks ostracized during and after school—she was miserable and humiliated. Until, that is, another girl broke a cardinal rule of the Girl Code and became its latest victim. Krista likens this cruel process to the movie *The Ring,* where viewers of the cursed film can save themselves by transferring their death sentences to others.

In a piece for *Thought Catalog,* Heather Thompson Day, a writer and lecturer at Southwestern Michigan College, recalls a similar experience. During high school, she and her friends publicly shunned another friend who had slept with her ex-boyfriend. The girl begged for forgiveness, but all attempts at reconciliation were disregarded. The humiliation and heartbreak was so painful for her, she ended up moving away. Years later, as a remorseful adult, Heather realized the girl's actions weren't rooted in cruel intentions, but rather a very human desire to feel wanted. "At sixteen, when a popular, handsome, teenage boy says all the right things, girls often do what they think they have to to make sure they don't stop," she wrote. Then another jarring realization emerges: she and that girl, "probably aren't that different."

Unfortunately, neither the cattiness nor the shunning ends after high school. If you've ever flipped through your social media feeds and come across evidence of a fun group outing that you never got an invite to, then you know this is true—and you also know that being left out is excruciating at any age.

Also notice how many tenets of Girl Code enforce specific rules related to mating. This is not a coincidence. A recent academic paper published in the fancy-sounding journal *Philosophical Transactions of the Royal Society B* finds, "For the most part, young women's competition is, directly or indirectly, about men and the resources they can provide. Hence it is perhaps unsurprising that women compete about those qualities that are highly valued by men: youth and attractiveness."

We've all seen this classic trope play out in every teen drama. Two girls—best friends since they were in diapers—both fall for the same boy. Oh no! But this isn't just a fictional storyline. Fighting over a mate is a curse of many real-life friendships, including one of my own.

Lily and I have been the closest of friends since the seventh grade, ever since she invited me to join her for lunch at the cool kids' table. (Lily has always been my gateway into anything cool.) There has only been one thing that has ever gotten between us in our more than twenty years of friendship: Brandon. Lily and I had never been interested in the same guy before. She preferred outgoing men with nice shoes, physical strength, and artistic talent, while I was more into gangly, emo types who wrote bad poetry in tiny notebooks and didn't have any upper body strength. Yet somehow our conflicting preferences collided during freshman year of college when we met Brandon. The irony, of course, was that Brandon didn't quite embody any of these traits, but still managed to attract both of our attention. He was decent enough, attractive enough, and nice enough. Nothing extraordinary, but for nearly two weeks, he caused an extraordinary rift in my relationship with Lily that left us both questioning if we'd ever speak to each other again. In the end, it turned out Brandon wasn't particularly interested in either one of us. (We later heard he dated a guy on Lily's floor.) And both Lily and I vowed never to allow a guy to get in the way of our friendship again—a promise that we have both kept for more than a decade.

Not all friendships survive these romantic situations. "I've witnessed hundreds, maybe thousands [of] female friendships get completely destroyed by a man," writes Emily Blackwood on the relationship site YourTango. "Whether it's a guy trying to sleep with two best friends or a girl who never feels noticed secretly resenting her magnetic bestie, romantic relationships kill platonic ones nearly every time."

The scientific name for this BFF killer is called intrasexual competition, and it's genetically programmed in all of us.

BACHELOR NATION: THE WOMEN TELL ALL

If you haven't brushed up on Darwin's theory of sexual selection, not to worry—intrasexual competition, in a nutshell, is *The Bachelor* franchise. All the terrible, yet titillating ways men and women fight, undermine, and backstab their own kind to win the affection of someone they have known for eight minutes is like watching evolution in real-time.

In this battle royal within the sexes, no weapons are off limits. Plenty of studies show that both genders will go to any lengths necessary, whether it be self-promotion, sabotage, or manipulation, to take home that group date rose. Of course, men and women approach this challenge differently. Men tend to rely heavily on bragging (or humble bragging), peacocking their possessions and resources: *See my flashy car! Try out my smart brain!* Whereas women will most often leverage their appearance: *Look! Boobs! Butts! Shiny hair!* A quick review of the number of breast implants and (dubious) dye jobs during twenty-one seasons of *The Bachelor* prove as much.

Men and women also utilize different tactics to screw over their rivals. Men like to diminish or undercut one another's achievements, status, or physical appearance. During JoJo Fletcher's season (*The Bachelorette*, Season 12), villain Chad Johnson regularly scared the spray tan right off the other men's thin skin with his aggressive, ego-busting, alpha dick behavior. And echoed throughout every season there seems to be the inevitable chorus of vilifying accusations ("He's not here for the right reasons!"), planting seeds of doubt for every bachelorette. *Is he here for me or Instagram followers?*

This is not to say women are above attacking each other's physical appearances. In seventh grade, the Regina George (the meanest, obviously prettiest girl from the 2004 film *Mean Girls*) of my school marched up to me and told me to my face, "You'd be pretty if you wore makeup." Women just have a different, deadlier weapon of choice: slut shaming. (After all, the only thing worse than being called ugly is being called a slut, amirite?) Through his research, evolutionary psychologist David Buss finds women are much more likely than men to attack another woman's sexuality, usually by spreading rumors about her sexual history or making nasty comments about her "revealing" clothing. Want proof? Just look at social media. A 2016 study by think tank Demos indicates that half of all misogynistic tweets, which contained the words "whore" or "slut," came from women themselves.

Corinne Olympios, the doe-eyed sexpot of Nick Viall's run (*The Bachelor, Season 21*) was subjected to this very treatment and deemed the franchise's sluttiest slut ever. Throughout the season, she was criticized by contestants and viewers alike for her escalating immoral antics, like taking her top off during a sexy photoshoot, dolloping a semi-exposed breast with Reddi-wip, and bouncing on top of Nick in a bouncy castle. Naturally, the cameras were always eager to cut away to footage of the other ladies looking shocked and disgusted by her behavior. I admit, it's unusual to see a Bachelor contestant so publicly comfortable with her own nudity and sexuality, but did Corinne really deserve to be branded a slut?

If you're dating someone (or trying to marry someone!), isn't it reasonable to make sure you are sexually compatible? Would you really be comfortable committing to someone forever without first trying out their man-chandise? Anthropologist Helen Fisher would not only find Corinne's behavior completely normal, but she would also applaud her application of slow love.

Slut shaming doesn't just exist within the confines of titillating reality television. It happens all the time in real life, too. In one 2011 experiment, a team of psychology researchers at the University of Ottawa observed the reactions of straight female participants when another woman walked into the room. Half of the subjects encountered an attractive, conservatively dressed woman, while the other half saw the same woman dressed in a sexy, more revealing outfit. The "sexy" version of the woman was almost always immediately critiqued on arrival by the study participants. One participant even boldly interjected, "What the fuck is that?!?" while the sexy woman was still in the room.

Believe it or not, women ten thousand years ago would have had the exact same reaction. Is it because deep down every woman is a mean girl? No, of course not . . . although we do have the capacity to be, especially when it comes to mating. Evolutionary theory states the most menacing threat to women seeking long-term relationships are women who aren't seeking them. If a man is offered no-strings-attached casual sex with a woman, he will be less incentivized and motivated to commit to a long-term relationship. Now it becomes clear why the The Bachelor contestants and the women from the previous experiment reacted as harshly they did. Even though no one was having sex with anyone, the overt sexuality of Corinne and the provocatively dressed woman in the study had the same effect. Which bring us to why women will weaponize a rival's sexuality. Thanks to the sexist double standard that just won't die, some men still expect the pasts of their sexual partners to be absent of any sex (or at least contain less sex than theirs), so when this chastity is put into question, so is the relationship.

NO POACHING ALLOWED

Did you know there are almost nineteen different ways women will try to poach or lure a man from another woman? The Bachelor has mastered most of them. Tactics range from infiltration through the guise of friendship to insidiously planting Inception-style seeds of doubt into the man about his current partner's fidelity or attractiveness. Though both men and women are poachers and can be poached, some researchers find men are more vulnerable to poaching. According to one comprehensive international study, which surveyed nearly 17,000 people around the world, 47 percent of American men have been successfully poached from a female partner, compared to 32 percent of American women from a male partner. And 15 percent of all current relationships are a result of poaching.

Even in imaginary, hypothetical scenarios, women seem to be more interested in attached men, according to an Oklahoma State University study that put this theory to the test. Researchers showed both straight male and female participants a photo of an attractive person of the opposite sex. Half of the participants were told that the person in the picture was single, while the other half were told the same person was in a relationship. As it turns out, 90 percent of female participants said they would be interested in pursuing a relationship with the attached man compared to just 59 percent who were interested in the single version of him. For men, however, it made no difference whether the woman pictured was attached or single. Their attraction remained the same. To explain why this happened, study author Melissa Burkley refers to a psychological theory called the "wedding ring effect." This theory suggests women are drawn to men who are partnered because they are seen as already having been vetted and appraised by someone else as a "good catch." It's the same reason why we vote for politicians who are endorsed by other politicians or organizations we admire. In the animal kingdom, this effect is known as mate choice copying, and has been observed among fish and bird species.

Though these studies seem to imply that single women are hardwired to homewreck, many of us (the nice ones, at least) will not act on these impulses. In the *Encyclopedia of Human Relationships*, Harry Reis and Susan Sprecher write, "Agreeable and conscientious people are less likely to be poachers than are unreliable and self-described erotophilic people (i.e., people who have positive feelings and responses to sex and sex-related stimuli)."

But let's say worse-case scenario, you do become the victim of a drive-by mate poaching, *now what?* Do you cry yourself to sleep every night and plot sweet revenge against the other woman and the ex that did this to you? You might not have to. Because the new couple is doomed to fail anyway. As Reis and Sprecher put it, "neurotic, unloving, and masculine people are more likely to be successfully poached away from an existing relationship." Not surprising, considering they were likely not the most doting or loyal of partners to begin with. Further, one 2004 international study found relationships where one partner was poached from another were more dysfunctional and less likely to last than those that were not—after all, what's to stop an easily poachable lover from being lured away again? As an example, take a look at just about any Hollywood romance.

More than a decade has passed since the Bennifer to Brangelina poaching scandal, yet people (on Twitter) still can't grasp why the tomb raider had to raid another woman's happy household. Why does a wildly successful, beautiful, wealthy, and talented superstar like Angelina Jolie need to pursue a married man when there are around sixty million single suitors out there who would easily saw off body parts for a chance to be in the same room with her. *Simple.* No one in that sixty million is a millionaire A-List superstar with an Academy Award, a Golden Globe, production company, and not one, but two, "sexiest man alive" covers for *People.* Not one of those sixty million are in her league. Brad Pitt, however, is.

Even regular, everyday women like me find themselves in a similar situation. While there is no shortage of men in the world, including single ones, the number of them I'd actually like to suck face and grow old with are few and far between. Do you know anyone who is so sick of all the intelligent, attractive, and all-around amazing guys always asking her out? Unlikely. This isn't only my observation either. Financial and tech journalist Jon Birger wrote an entire book about this so-called man deficit, *Date-Onomics: How Dating Became a Lopsided Numbers Game*. The lopsided number he is referring to is the shortage of college-educated men compared to college-educated women. Across most parts of the US, there are just three college-educated men for every four college-educated women. Because many women prefer to date partners with a comparable educational background, a man with a diploma is considered very much in demand. Being a hot commodity comes with many perks, of course. Average-looking dopes suddenly get VIP access to way more attractive babes. In this economy, men are the buyers and women are the sellers, and it's a buyer's market, which as Birger describes, "turn some nice guys into monsters." He interviewed one such "average-looking guy" turned monster, who upon moving to New York in his mid-twenties, quickly discovered the ease of disposing girlfriends like plastic utensils:

> "At one point, I was dating someone who was by far the most attractive woman—and by far the most sexually adventurous woman—I'd ever dated, and I broke up with her because I knew I could find someone just as wild but maybe a little bit smarter. A year or two before, it would have been inconceivable for me to even be with someone that hot and that sexy—never mind for me to break up with her."

DO WOMEN EXPECT TOO MUCH FROM EACH OTHER?

The other day, my friend Lisa warned me she probably wouldn't see me for the next several months because she was going to be a bridesmaid . . . again. As this was going to be her tenth time bestowed with the honor, she was by now very familiar with her expected duties and their associated costs. On average, a member of a wedding party spends around $1,500, according to a *U.S. News* report. To me, this is already a jaw-dropping amount, so when she told me she had already spent double that, just on accommodations and travel to the destination wedding venue (bridal shower, bachelorette party, hair and makeup, bridesmaid dress, and bridal gifts not included), I was shocked. She, on the other hand, had been down this route so many times before that she didn't even seem to notice. To decline the honor, she told me, was impossible, unthinkable even. For Lisa and many other cash-strapped bridesmaids I talked to, saying "thanks, but no thanks" to being a bridesmaid is tantamount to irrevocably destroying the friendship. "You can't say no to your best friend," she says. Apparently, not even when they're trying to bankrupt you.

Lisa's situation reminds me of the Girl Code and the burdensome expectations that women, sometimes unwittingly, have of their girlfriends. This is especially true when it comes to the myriad obligations tied to weddings. Just compare the number of magazine articles aimed at teaching women how to inoffensively say no to being a bridesmaid compared to similar advice for groomsmen. None of this surprises Eileen Kennedy-Moore, a psychologist and the author of *Growing Friendships: A Kids' Guide to Making and Keeping Friends*. Even from a young age, she told me, "girls expect more from their friendships and become more upset when they violate expectations." It is common knowledge that the way women befriend each other is different from that of men. Women bond emotionally—laughing, crying, and shit-talking—whereas men connect physically—guzzling, high-fiving, and roughhousing. Women need friends who are dependable and loyal. Men don't like friends who need anything. Which is likely why women tend to be cattier and hold more grudges against each other than men, according to Geoffrey Greif, author of *Buddy System*.

Just like any set of rules and regulations, the Girl Code is designed not only to protect friendships, but also to maintain law and order. Of course, not everyone enjoys being governed by them. Both Lisa and my earlier dinner companions have all experienced their share of PTSD moments where the rules or their enforcement have either hurt or harmed them.

But, as much as women fight or get angry with one another, research indicates they might still be better off than men, women tend to be more invested in maintaining their friendships than men and they are also more intimate and supportive of each other. Over the past two decades, my best friend Lily and I have had our share of disagreements and tiffs (e.g., Brandon) yet we always seem to find a way to return to one another. While I wouldn't go so far as to say that each argument reinforces the foundation of our friendship, it does motivate both of us to be more cognizant of what drives the other person crazy, which does help us avoid future conflicts.

And while friendship is valuable for both men and women, studies find ladies reap far more benefits from their buds—both emotional and physical. In fact, one University of California study found that female cancer patients who had friends were four times more likely to recover than women who had none. Interestingly, having a spouse did not affect a patient's likelihood of survival. Having close friends is so essential for women that Harvard Medical School researchers compare not having any pals as "detrimental to your health as smoking or carrying extra weight."

For me this is very true. During either celebration or tragedy, Lily and my closest girlfriends have been my most spirited champions and my life support. I would never have made it this far in life (or written this chapter) without them. Though our Girl Code rules do occasionally cause trauma, irritation, and exaggerated eye rolls, they also ensure continued loyalty, support, and trust—through thick and thin—from some of the best people I know. I suspect this is why so many of us simply suck it up and do our best to follow all the thousands—or millions—of rules that help us keep these friends in our lives.

Chapter 10
Love and . . . Everyone Else

Why other people will always make us feel like a complete failure.

Pinterest, like farting, is one of those silent, but deadly relationship killers. Not just a site for crafting enthusiasts and delicious recipes, it has become the premiere go-to destination for FOMO (fear of missing out), thanks to an endless scroll of aspirational wedding, home, and lifestyle fantasies. Obviously, having a regular low-budget wedding won't do, not when someone on Pinterest deforested twenty acres to erect a barnyard made of rare Burmese teak for her twenty-minute ceremony. When you look at what everyone else is doing—and trust me, they are doing really amazing things—you can't help but feel like a failure. And, if you're in a relationship, it's difficult not to take some of that frustration out on your partner. See examples below.

Why don't we have a washer and dryer like them? Why do we still only buy IKEA furniture? Why haven't you recruited sixty of our closest friends for a flash mob to learn a professionally choreographed dance and propose to me in a viral video?

What our partners consider mind-numbing nagging might actually be a lesson in social priming, or how external cues unconsciously influence our behavior. Every human being living on Earth is influenced by outside factors, including, but not limited to: social taboos, cultural norms, human beings in close proximity, other human beings outside of close proximity, film and television, *Us Weekly*, FOX News, cat videos, and social media posts featuring the world's most obnoxious couples. These types of outside factors work in incognito mode to shape how we think, behave, and go about our daily routines, according to social psychologist John Bargh, who came to this conclusion in the early 1990s after conducting a series of breakthrough experiments. Bargh and his research team tasked two groups of participants to create sentences using different sets of words. The control group all got words that were random, whereas the test group were given words like: "bingo," "Florida," "worried," "bitter," and "retired," which bring to mind very specific imagery of a curmudgeonly senior citizen in Bermuda shorts yelling at kids to get off his lawn. The researchers wanted to know if exposure to the aging-themed words would influence participants' subsequent behavior, so they timed how quickly it took both groups of participants to walk down a hallway after they created their sentences. It turned out that the words did have a bit of a *13 Going on 30* effect. On average, the Floridian-worded group walked slower than the control group. The researchers also conducted similar experiments, including one where test subjects were primed with rude words. Once again, life imitated vocabulary, as those in the rude word group were significantly more likely to interrupt a conversation than those primed with polite or neutral words. So isn't it entirely possible that these happy couples on Pinterest, with their fancy washing machines and Room & Board furniture, were making me unconsciously feel like I should have these things, too?

Or maybe my jealousy is all conscious and calculated. Maybe I know exactly what I'm doing. Which leads us to social comparison theory.

WE NEED TO TALK ABOUT SOCIAL COMPARISON THEORY

Baked into each of our big, beautiful brains is an innate human need to define ourselves and our worth. And, most of the time, the best and only option we have to evaluate our life performance is to compare it against someone else's. This is the key principle of social comparison theory, and it completely goes against my mother's No. 2 rule of life: "Don't compare yourself to anyone else." (In case you're curious, the No. 1 rule is: "Take a jacket. It's going to get cold later.") Unfortunately, trying not to compare yourself to other people is a lot like trying to breathe underwater—it's impossible.

Though social comparison theory sounds like a recent discovery born on someone's Instagram feed, it was actually developed long before the social media revolution in 1954 by Leon Festinger, a renowned social psychologist of the era. To Festinger, why we compare ourselves is as important as who we compare ourselves to. Just as that thief Goldilocks preferred soup that wasn't too hot or too cold, we are equally picky about who we measure ourselves against—our competitors have to be just right! He explains in his groundbreaking thesis, "A person does not tend to evaluate his opinions or his abilities by comparison with others who are too divergent from himself." This means I probably shouldn't draw parallels between that one time I participated in a beach cleanup and the accomplishments of Nobel Peace Prize winner and human rights activist Malala Yousafzai or my strictly drunken karaoke-only singing abilities to the pipes of Adele.

But once we do find appropriate and comparable peers who are not way out of our league (or just a little out of our league), there are two types of social comparison we can engage in, upward or downward. As the name suggests, upward comparisons occur when we measure our abilities against someone we think is somewhat better, luckier, or more loved by God than us. More people make upward comparisons which, as you might guess results in feelings of burnout, defeat, jealousy, and inferiority. Although, some annoying overachievers argue that there are certain advantages to making these lofty comparisons, believing that having more successful peers can actually motivate you to perform better or push you closer to your goals.

I am not one of these people.

When possible, my preferred direction to peer at my peers is down. I would rather compare myself to people I consider worse off than myself. The cast of *Jersey Shore*, people who leave angry comments on the Internet, or Jared, my third-grade classmate who used to stare at me while he ate pencils in class are a few folks that come to mind. Whenever I'm feeling down, I think of these misfits and say to myself, "Well, at least I'm not *[fill in the blank]*," and immediately feel better about my own life. In general, the scientific community feels the same way. Multiple studies have found downward comparisons tend to increase well-being, elicit feelings of gratitude, and give our egos a nice boost. Unfortunately, the effects, like Botox, are only temporary.

Though most people are guilty of comparing themselves to others, some of us do it far more than we should. Remember, everything in moderation. Especially since neither type of comparison is particularly good for you or your self-esteem. If you're happy and you know it, don't compare yourself. In her 2001 paper, *Why Are Some People Happier Than Others?* researcher Sonja Lyubomirsky finds that unhappy or depressed people are more susceptible to making comparisons or being affected by them than their happier counterparts. In one of her experiments, students earned praise or criticism for a task, and then heard a peer receive either better or worse feedback for doing the same task. As you can imagine, both happy and unhappy students reported feeling great when they received more praise than their peers, but only unhappy students were royally pissed when their peers got better feedback than they did. In fact, unhappy students were so sensitive to their peers' performance, that they reported feeling happier and more self-confident when they had received a *bad* evaluation (but heard their peer got an even worse one) than when they had received an *excellent* evaluation (but heard their peer received an even better one.) This is the equivalent of saying, *I'm happy to be stupid as long as you are stupider than me.*

Maybe misery doesn't love company after all. Misery only loves company that is more miserable.

Further delving into the dark and destructive side of social comparisons is a 2006 study published in the *Journal of Adult Development* in which researchers asked a group of adults how often they compared themselves to others and whether they felt certain negative emotions, such as guilt, regret, envy, and having unmet cravings. As to be expected, the results again illustrated a direct correlation between making frequent social comparisons and negative feelings.

IS SHE PRETTIER THAN ME?

Whenever one of my exes gets a new girlfriend (don't ask me how I know, I just do), I find a picture of her (again, don't ask), which I urgently text to one of my best friends asking: IS SHE PRETTY?!?

The truth is I'm not really asking if she is pretty. I'm asking if she is prettier *than me.* Welcome to social comparison theory 101 for females.

Close your eyes and imagine a world where an entire gender has been taught their entire lives to believe that their worth is tied to their physical appearance. Just kidding, you don't have to imagine it, you're living it. Don't believe me? Look at the $56.2 billion beauty industry, whose entire business model is to convince you that you should look like someone else. Or consider the 15.9 million plastic surgeries that took place in 2015—the No. 1 being breast augmentation. When has anyone ever *needed* bigger breasts? Why are women seven times more likely to have an eating disorder than men? Who do you think the $200 billion weight-loss industry is targeting when they recruit celebrities like Oprah (and pay her $70 million) to promote the benefits of calorie counting and bland, tasteless food? (Hint: look in the mirror.) Remember in 2011, when Diet Pepsi launched its now defunct "skinny can"—a "taller, sassier" version of the regular can at Fashion Week with actress Sofia Vergara at the helm of its print campaign? No? Good, because the demoralizing campaign was crushed almost as soon as it hit the mainstream, but not before reinforcing the idea that a woman must be defined by her physical weight. In fact, women are so traumatized by their weight (or the expectations of how much they are supposed to weigh) that 46 percent of them said they would be willing to give up a year of their life rather than be obese, according to a 2006 Yale

University study. Even more incredible is the fact that 15 percent of the women surveyed admitted they would be willing to sacrifice ten years. There's nothing new or particularly interesting about how society and pop culture perpetuate unrealistic standards of beauty. Today, we may covet the combo of Kim Kardashian's tiny waist and voluptuous derriere, but in the '90s, it was all about "the Rachel" haircut, a regrettable layered do that was ultimately a *do not* and took forever to grow out. A century earlier, the Gibson Girl was considered the paradigm of femininity, with her slimly drawn figure and large boobs, a look only realistically achieved by giving up independent breathing and wearing an extremely tight corset.

Each time we beautify or starve ourselves, we expect it will change our entire lives, but it rarely does. Instead, we wait for the next fad to show us that we're still not quite where we should be.

SOCIAL MEDIA IS DESTROYING MY SOUL

When was the last time you logged onto Facebook and felt really great and pleased with how things were going in your life? If you can't remember (or if this has never happened), you're not alone. This is because (How do I say this tactfully?) social media is destroying our souls. Numerous researchers have linked heavy social media usage to depression, anxiety, and low self-esteem, particularly for young adults in their twenties and early thirties.

Which can be a major problem, since the average adult spends nearly two hours daily scrolling through other people's lives online. This is still nothing compared to teenagers, however, who treat social media like a full-time job, devoting up to nine hours of their day to a networking site. It seems the most obvious solution to put ourselves out of this self-imposed misery would be to quit cold turkey, an experiment that the Denmark-based think tank Happiness Research Institute conducted on 1,095 test subjects in 2015. During what was dubbed "The Facebook Experiment," researchers asked participants to go on a one-week moratorium from the social networking site. At the end of the week— to no one's surprise—everyone who successfully accomplished this impressive feat reported a significantly higher level of overall life satisfaction, and everyone who failed continued to be miserable.

My own feelings toward social media are predictably complicated. One clear advantage of being perpetually online is that it facilitates faster and easier connection with people, particularly those who have different backgrounds and life experiences than yours. You can establish an intimate bond with a stranger across the world via one shared hashtag. There's also those addictive sixty-second

Tasty cooking videos which make me feel like a Michelin-starred chef without so much as turning on an oven. And memes. Of course, memes. These are the greeting cards of the Internet, with an uncanny ability to articulate our personal brand of snark and passive-aggression better than we ever could. All of these by-products of social media are certainly nice to have; the only downside is that it is also robbing me of my will to live.

In the famous Internet Paradox study of the late 1990s, Carnegie Mellon researchers had already figured all of this out. Back then, the Internet was just a no-man's-land of "You've got mail!" greetings and group chat rooms, but still the researchers knew that being online led to reduced family communication, less friends, depression, and loneliness. Fast-forward to 2017, when a University of Pittsburgh study reconfirms the findings of the Internet Paradox and also presents a new chicken-and-egg conundrum: Were lonely people initially drawn to social media, or did social media use make people lonely? It's an interesting question—one that researchers are hard at work trying to figure out—but does it really matter when all of us are already trapped in its vicious cycle?

I WISH I KNEW HOW TO QUIT YOU

How do you give up something as powerful, all-knowing, and designed to tap into your psyche as social media so astutely does? The first step in Alcoholics Anonymous is to admit your powerlessness over alcohol and that it has made you lose control over your life. So here goes nothing: *Hi, my name is Jen, and I'm a social media addict.*

We must come to terms with the fact that social media is designed to be addictive, and as a *Computerworld* piece describes, "engineered to be as habit-forming as crack cocaine." Part of what makes social networking so tantalizingly addictive is the 2011 runner-up to word of the year: FOMO (fear of missing out). There are 1.23 billion users on Facebook worldwide. I personally know a dozen dogs who are active on Facebook. Everyone and their mom is on Facebook, *literally*. And many of these people (and animals) are constantly sharing important news and life-changing memes that you are unable to access without first logging on. Not to mention, evil engineers and data scientists are always hard at work, scheming new and nefarious tactics to turn us into lab rats craving likes, views, and skin-beautifying filters for pellets of emotional nourishment. Algorithms curate an endless scroll of irresistible content. Every new friend request produces an immediate ego boost and a shot of insatiable curiosity. The entire tech industry is working to own your eyeballs, and for many of us, they already do.

In 2015, researchers at Cornell University studied Facebook addiction in 5,000 subjects, who pledged to give up the social media platform for ninety-nine days. As to be expected, some people fell off the wagon, but these shortcomings still helped researchers paint a portrait of the kind of person who decided to return to Facebook or stay off for good, based on the following four primary indicators.

1. **Perceived addiction**: Participants who believed social media was more addictive or habit-forming were more likely to revert back to use.
2. **Privacy:** Those who did not like Facebook's surveillance policy were not as likely to return, whereas those who use "Facebook largely to manage how other people think of them are more likely to log back in."
3. **Subjective mood:** If you were in a good mood, you were less likely to log back in. (This supports the previous research, which suggests happy people don't need to compare themselves to others.)
4. **Other social media:** Those who had other social media profiles, such as Twitter or Instagram, were less likely to return. And even if they did, many would alter their use or change their habits. For example, they might delete the app from their phone or schedule certain times to go on it.

THE DELICIOUS TASTE OF SCHADENFREUDE

The other day, I received a shocking text from a friend that read: *Guess which asshole got engaged?* Obviously, there are a lot of assholes in my life, but my magical gut intuition already knew who it was. Our former coworker, Simon, a textbook asshole (but not the attractive or charming kind) had just announced his engagement to a size 00 Brazilian bikini model on Facebook in a pithy 5,000-word essay, supplemented with staged photos of a beachside tropical paradise, a blindingly enormous ring, and requisite champagne toast. Hallmark-card-ripped phrases, such as *found my soul mate, stunningly beautiful, happiest man in the world*, were strategically inserted throughout the post. Turning your social media into a makeshift *New York Times* wedding announcement is nothing original. And believe it or not, these celebratory declarations (e.g., I got engaged!, I had twins!!, I ate three donuts!!!) don't bother me. *Correction:* They don't bother me as long as they come from people I like.

Simon did not fall into this category. Because his father owned the business we worked at, he felt compelled to treat everyone like his personal assistant, and once even referred to me as "the assistant." I didn't even have a name. He once called my pen a "piece of shit." *My pen!* For the record, it wasn't a piece of shit. It was a rolling ball pen that cost $3, but that's the kind of piece of shit he was. Despite his lackluster looks and personality, his office always looked like a casting session for a Victoria's Secret commercial—a harem of beautiful women ready to answer his every beck and call.

Ever the fool, I assumed I had left all my rage against him in the past. But like the North, the Internet never forgets. Thanks to social media, past traumas eagerly await to be resurrected so they can haunt us time and time again with every scroll of the timeline. Instead of deleting the text and forgetting about it and that horrible chapter in my life *(yeah, right)*, I logged onto Facebook and pored over both his and his new fiancée's profiles, desperately searching for a single shred of evidence that would tell me that his life was not as irritatingly perfect as it seemed. Did I really live in a world where this asshole travels first-class on his family's dime and marries the girl of his dreams? Do assholes really win? This is the kind of bizarro reality Marty McFly gets trapped in *Back to the Future Part II*, not me.

There had to be something, anything, incriminating—a photo of the bikini model looking like she ate carbohydrates, a passive-aggressive status update suggesting trouble brewing in paradise. But hours into the investigation, all I managed to recover was an array of colored heart emojis, an album of couples' selfies straight out of *Travel and Leisure,* and a gnawing sense that the universe was indeed more unfair that I had initially imagined. In my bloodthirst for schaden-freude, it seemed I had come up empty-handed . . . *for now.*

Schadenfreude is the German word for getting off on another person's misery. *Schaden* literally means "harm," and *freude* means "joy." Though the word first appeared in the Oxford English Dictionary in 1982, it was introduced to the non-German speaking mainstream a decade earlier by Thomas Pynchon in his novel, *Gravity's Rainbow*, which described this harmful joy as an exclusively German trait. Several decades prior, the British publication *The Spectator* had also suggested, "There is no English word for schadenfreude, because there is no such feeling here."

Yeah, right. Any zealous sports fan watching their rivals lose will tell you other-wise. Or the scientists who studied them will.

Why does it feel so good to see people we despise experience misfortune? As it turns out, schadenfreude does actually trigger feelings of happiness in our brains, according to a 2011 study at Princeton University. Neuroscientists analyzed the brains of die-hard Red Sox and Yankees fans as they watched clips from broadcasted baseball games and found the region associated with plea-sure—the ventral striatum—lit up whenever their favorite players hit a home run or when the rival team struck out. Interestingly, the scientists noted the fans who experienced the most pleasure in response to the rival team's failures also showed the most aggression.

In fact, the happiness we feel when an asshole gets just what he deserves is akin to real happiness. In a 2015 German study, scientists used electromyography to record the facial expressions created by four different emotions: arousal, joy, schadenfreude, and sadness. The results indicated no physically distinguishable difference between joy and schadenfreude.

Even sweet, angelic little babies show pleasure when someone they don't like experiences harm, according to a study published in *Psychological Science*, which observed the behavior of nine- and fourteen-month-old infants. For one of the experiments, the babies indicated to researchers their favorite snack—either green beans or graham crackers—and then watched a puppet show where one of two bunny puppets shared the same snack preference. The babies then watched additional puppet shows, featuring one of the two bunny puppets and a new dog puppet that would act as either a "helper" or a "harmer" when the bunny dropped the ball. The helper would retrieve the ball and return it to the bunny, while the harmer would take the ball and run. During these shows, the babies preferred the dog puppet who helped the bunny with similar tastes—yet also preferred the dog puppet who harmed the bunny with the snack preference different from them. (Does this explain why I don't trust people who like Thou-sand Island dressing?)

Learning this is what inspired me to compile a brief list of situations where schadenfreude may be petty, but still completely appropriate:

- When the guy who unceremoniously dumped you in turn gets unceremo-niously dumped by someone else.
- When the Regina George of your middle school or high school turns out to be painfully average as an adult.
- When the person who stole the parking space you were clearly waiting for can't open her car door because the curb is too high and she has to crawl out the passenger side.
- When that narcissist dick you used to work with (finally) gets dumped by his Brazilian model fiancée.

BREAKING NEWS: EVERYTHING YOU READ ON THE INTERNET IS A LIE

Instagram is *Lifestyles of the Rich and Famous* for the twenty-first century. As you thumb through an endless feed of enviably beautiful people with beautiful skin who are all on permanent vacation, it's easy to imagine Robin Leach narrating each hashtag in his fancy British accent. But the truth, as debt collectors have recently discovered, is that these filtered photos represent little more than a literal scroll of lies. This fraudulent attempt to keep up with the Joneses was featured in a *Wall Street Journal* story, which detailed how bankruptcy asset hunters went after chapter 7 bankruptcy filers "posing in glamorous-looking jewelry, piloting boats and ATVs, and even displaying buckets full of cash" on social media only to discover that these items were fakes or did not belong to them. Even ostensibly wealthy celebrities, like 50 Cent, have been guilty of selling this fantasy to their followers. In 2016, an Instagram photo of the rapper posing with wads of cash was revealed to be fake, after the judge hearing his bankruptcy case questioned him about these undisclosed assets.

Nearly two-thirds of everyone on social media lies on their profiles in order to make their lives appear more appealing, according to a 2015 British survey, which makes a lot of sense considering the same survey also finds more than 75 percent of respondents admit to judging their peers based on what they post on their social media channels. Ironically, in the bizarro world of social media, lying somehow makes people feel less lame. However, what is most disconcerting is another study which finds that 16 percent of young people only recall the social media version of their lives, meaning they cannot accurately recall their actual memories.

This is not to say that social media exclusively breeds a petri dish of lies, but it certainly doesn't incentivize telling the truth. Why post close-ups of our cellulite, back fat, and stained underwear when we can easily Photoshop or filter the flaws away?

DO RELATIONSHIPS SUFFER WHEN EVERYONE IS UP IN YOUR BUSINESS?

Unlike most people I know, I have always been reticent to reveal any aspect of my love life on social media. Not once have I ever changed my profile photo to a cute couples photo or left a gushy comment on a significant other's posts. It's not that I don't want to—I just don't want to deal with the aftermath of what happens if or when the relationship ends. *You know what I'm talking about.* Once your relationship goes public, everyone gets up in your business. Whether you're celebrating your six-month anniversary at The Cheesecake Factory or breaking up the day before Valentine's Day, Facebook and the gang are always there to offer their unsolicited opinions on all of it.

Inviting all the virtual people in your life to pry into your relationship is asking for a situation akin to those sitcoms like *Everybody Loves Raymond*, where nosy, annoying in-laws instigate havoc in a couple's business. And just as television parents cause friction in a couple's relationship, so do Facebook peers, according to researchers at the University of Missouri-Columbia, who analyzed eighteen- to eighty-two-year-olds on their Facebook use and romantic relationships. They found newer couples who engaged in excessive Facebook use were more likely to experience fighting, cheating, breakups, and divorce scenarios than those who didn't, which shouldn't come as a shock, since Facebook is a gateway to notorious relationship killers, like reconnecting with exes, outbreaks of jealousy and paranoia, and FOMO. Of course, this kind of trouble usually brews behind the scenes, so your viewers only see what you curate for them, i.e., a manufactured romance filled with cropped photos of holding hands and giant bouquets of flowers captioned #justbecause.

For a long time, I believed these lies. I would scroll through hundreds of photos, wondering, *Can this kind of perfect couple truly exist?* Not really, according to science. A 2014 study published in the *Personality and Social Psychology Bulletin* finds that people who are always making a huge deal out of their relationships are usually the most insecure about them: "On a daily basis, when people felt more insecure about their partner's feelings, they tended to make their relationship visible." Overcompensating affection on social media (or otherwise) doesn't work to save your relationship, no matter how many mushy status updates you post.

SNL legend Lorne Michaels said of comedy, "The problem with making it look easy is that people think it's easy!" The same could be said for relationships on social media. And, because it looks so effortless, we demand a similarly seamless experience in our own lives. Pinterest, too, with its ostensibly attainable gallery of DIY hairstyles and crafts does an Oscar-worthy performance of making you believe that you can create an artistic masterpiece with just a used toothbrush, some coconut oil, and fingernail clippings. Google "Epic Pinterest Fails" and you'll see just how unbelievably easy it is to carefully follow directions yet still end up with a pile of dog poo.

This is not to say all couples are fake and miserable on social media, obviously. And if you are one of those genuine couples who have reached true #relationshipgoals status, good for you! How did you do it? *Please tell me.*

GOODBYE, EVERYONE ELSE

In the end, our innate drive for competition is what keeps us alive. Hundreds of thousands of years ago, our ancestors climbed evolution's totem pole, not only by competing for the best mates and resources, but also by competing against nature and wildlife. Back then, self-worth was a reflection of our survival skills, unlike today, where it is determined by how many followers or likes we get. Both have their challenges. Photoshopping a convincing thigh gap in a picture may not be as difficult as outrunning a lion to avoid being dinner, but a misstep in either situation can prove unfavorable. Yes, the lion would like to kill you, but only for its own survival. The same cannot be said for the 24 percent of adults who readily admit to being Internet trolls—and the many more who don't admit to it.

No matter how much time, energy, or cash we devote to upgrading our lives, becoming skinnier, smarter, and *better* versions of ourselves, we still can't seem to be satisfied with what we achieve. And if it's not us, it's our moms who still want *better* for us. Everything in this chapter—actually, everything in this book—speaks to this insatiability. And this attitude is taking a toll on us. One self-esteem expert claims more than 85 percent of the population has low self-esteem, and is plagued by fear, failure, unfulfillment, frustration, and indecision. How often do we hear others (or ourselves, even) say, "I like you just as you are"? Probably not very often. Not only because no one really talks like that outside of the movies, but because we don't actually feel this way, which explains why finding and/or being in a healthy relationship feels so challenging at times.

Relationship experts and psychologists always warn us not to get into relationships until we love ourselves and are OK being alone, because it's "when you're in the right place" that the right person will come along, and other smart, but ultimately unrealistic, advice, at least for me. If I had waited until I loved myself—I mean, *truly loved myself*—before entering a relationship, then I would never have been in one. I wouldn't be in one now.

Which is why I wanted to write this book in the first place. I had to assume there were other confused, clueless people out there who, like me, were struggling to make sense of their world and their perplexing relationships. Those who also wonder why their romances don't end up like the ones flooding Instagram or featured in wedding blogs. This is not to say I have given up on love. *Not at all.* There is still nothing I desire more than to marry Ryan and start our new life together (except maybe score another book deal, just sayin'!). When I first set out researching this book, I imagined it would be so easy to hold my ancestors, my biology, nearly anything else, accountable for my inability to be in the relationships that I wanted and felt I deserved. And while there were plenty of studies to support these conclusions, I realized that simply knowing why we are the way we are doesn't really serve us. I mean, it's a very cool (or annoying) party trick to correctly guess what type of locus of control my friends have, but unless I'm shifting my own locus toward the internal, it really doesn't matter.

As it turns out, blaming everyone and everything else for my problems didn't make me feel better. During the months that it took to write this book, two friends got married, four got engaged, three got pregnant (two with their second child), and one gave birth. Now I have two choices: I can revert to my default mode, where I allow social comparisons and my external locus get the better of me as I whine and lecture Ryan on the fragile state of my ostensibly doomed fertility—or I can remind myself that these feelings of inferiority and inability to reach important life milestones are mostly manufactured by archaic social standards. That my jealousy is real, but may be (temporarily) quelled by a good oxytocin-infused hug. And that when it comes to love, whether it be for someone else or myself, the answer may not always be simple, but that doesn't mean I won't find it.

Epilogue
Are My Favorite TV Couples Still Together?

What happens when reality infiltrates happily ever after.

Like many children of the '80s and '90s, I learned how to live through television. That my family and friends didn't look or behave like anyone on my favorite shows was irrelevant. I did not consider them part of my "real" life anyways. My "real" parents were the hilariously and hip Alan and Amy Matthews from *Boy Meets World*. I even had a different set of best friends for every day of the week. For instance, on Saturdays I hung out with Lisa, Zack, Slater—and Jessie and Kelly, if they were permitted on-screen. Wednesdays were spent with Dawson, Pacey, and Joey—all of us taking turns ugly crying and practicing our SAT words.

In some cases, it's been a couple of decades since the demise of these shows, yet I still think about these characters who helped shape my views on relationships. Their teenage milestones mirrored mine, some of them anyway. I was there for their first kisses and their first heartbreaks. I was a key witness to when they wrecked their parents' car and when they later went to college. They even let me watch them lose their virginity to someone they barely knew, while the person they were really meant to be with was pining for them at home. Each week, I waited with bated breath to see what new catastrophe would disrupt their love lives, and by extension, mine.

In spite of the endless drama and obstacles, these teenage and young adult dramas always seemed to end with the proverbial happy ending. Because in TV land, unlike real life, that's what's supposed to happen. *But what about afterward? What did their lives look like after the cameras stopped rolling? What happens when every kiss no longer elicits an audience-generated OOOOHHHHH or romantic moment doesn't come with its own twinkly soundtrack? Where are these couples now?* (**Warning:** Imaginary spoilers ahead)

Boy Meets World (1993–2000)

Topanga and Corey

As they had never done anything independently of each other during the entire seven-year run of the show, Topanga, Corey, Shawn, and Eric all move to New York after the season finale. The foursome, plus two random roommates they find on Craigslist, share a 150-square-foot studio apartment in Queens—it's all they can afford, since no one except Topanga has any sort of income. Corey attempts stand-up comedy, but ultimately fails because he has zero work ethic and all of his jokes are about Mr. Feeny. Topanga considers leaving Corey, but ultimately stays with him once she learns that there are 38 percent more female college grads than men in New York and all her law school friends do is complain about the creeps and weirdos they meet online. Several years later, Corey and Topanga star in a television show based on their lives, along with their two precocious children, the older sibling exhibiting the same penchant for over-the-top hamminess as her father. The show gets canned after three seasons. Corey is currently unemployed.

Dawson's Creek (1998–2003)

Joey and Pacey

At the end of six seasons, Joey at last ends the show's agonizing love triangle and chooses former *Mighty Duck* Pacey over human Oompa Loompa Dawson. However, as soon as they begin dating in earnest, her doubt resurfaces. Eventually, she returns to Dawson, who immediately tosses out his Steven Spielberg sex doll in order to rekindle their romance. Still, Joey finds herself missing Pacey and rehashes the same story line from when they were kids, until the three of them finally decide to forego traditionally monogamy and embrace a polyamorous lifestyle, which ultimately better suits them. Today they all live on Pacey's boat, where they spend their free time reading the dictionary and watching Joey tuck her hair behind her ears.

Felicity (1998–2002)

Felicity and Ben

The series ends predictably with Noel marrying someone who is not Felicity, and Felicity giving Ben another chance. Despite Ben's earnest vow to never again cheat on Felicity, his problematic dreaminess continues to attract unwanted female attention, much to her dismay. Once again, Ben is unfaithful to Felicity, but instead of going to therapy or trying to resolve their relationship in a healthy, normal way, Felicity again resorts to witchcraft and travels back in time to see what would have happened had she chosen a different path. Except this time, she finds herself trapped in another alternate reality, one in which instead of following Ben to New York, she ends up attending Chico State University near Sacramento, California, where she is currently enrolled in the school's pre-med program and is desperately trying to locate her former roommate and witch, Meghan.

Friends (1994–2004)
Rachel and Ross

After a decade of bickering and star-studded cameo love interests, Ross and Rachel decide to give their relationship another shot in the series finale. This only lasts another twenty-two minutes before each one realizes that the other person is still a self-involved narcissist, and together they make the worst couple ever. They are still single when they reunite a decade later at Marcel the monkey's funeral. And despite hooking up again, they realize they are much better off as friends. They have not been in contact since.

My So-Called Life (1994–1995)
Angela and Jordan

Even though Angela finds out the Cyrano de Bergerac of her panty-dropping love letter is her nerdy, irascible neighbor Brian, the final shot still ends with her being led away by the illiterate, but devastatingly sexy frontman of the Frozen Embryos himself, Jordan Catalano. He drives them to school and breaks into their special spot for romance: the boiler room, while Brian goes home and sulks. Angela already realizes that she doesn't have a real future with Jordan, but it doesn't change the fact he is still the hottest person she has ever seen, let alone swapped spit with. Or that she is only fifteen, an age when the only thing that matters is being wanted by the right person. *Who cares if he can't read? Or cheated on you with your best friend? Or pressured you to have sex when you weren't ready?* Now, more than twenty years later, Angela writes for online sites, like *Medium* and *Thought Catalog,* where she waxes nostalgic about her idyllic adolescence. She is dating someone, but it's not serious. And every so often she finds herself searching for Jordan Catalano on Facebook, but always comes up empty-handed. She wonders if he ever does the same for her. (He doesn't, as he still hasn't learned how to read).

Saved By the Bell (1989–1993; 1994, if you count *Saved by the Bell: The College Years*, which I don't)

Kelly and Zack

Shortly after their $1,200 wedding in Vegas, which even their principal Mr. Belding attends, Zack and Kelly move to Los Angeles, where they are both encouraged to pursue careers in entertainment. Kelly finds moderate success, playing a vixen on a popular teen television show, and Zack becomes a correspondent on the television show *Extra,* where Slater also works. After the series ends, Kelly takes a break from acting and they have three kids, each better looking than the next. As Zack's career takes off, Kelly launches a mommy blog called *Zack&KellyPlus3,* where her assistant documents their idyllically curated life, along with the occasional sponsored post (but she swears she would promote these products even if she wasn't getting paid to). TLC offers the couple a reality show, where they mostly just try to relive their high school glory days, which gets canceled after the first episode. Today, Zack hosts *Extra* and is currently dating several women on *Ashley Madison,* while Kelly still runs her blog and is a cast member of *The Real Housewives of Beverly Hills.* They haven't had sex in four years.

Bibliography

CHAPTER 1

Smith, Aaron and Anderson, Monica. "5 facts about online dating." Pew Research Center. February 29, 2016. Accessed June 1, 2017. http://www.pewresearch. org/fact-tank/2016/02/29/5-facts-about-online-dating/.

Schwartz, Barry. *The Paradox of Choice: Why More Is Less.* New York: Harper Perennial, 2004.

Helliwell, J.; Layard, R.; and Sachs, J. World Happiness Report 2017, New York: Sustainable Development Solutions Network. 2017.

Wiking, Meik. *The Little Book of Hygge: The Danish Way to Live Well.* London: Penguin Life, 2016.

MacLellan, Lila. "The happiness of the Danes can easily be explained by 10 cultural rules." Quartz. September 29, 2016. Accessed June 1, 2017. https: //qz.com/794740/the-happiness-of-the-danes-can-easily-be-explained-by- 10-cultural-rules/.

Ansari, Aziz and Klinenberg, Eric. *Modern Romance.* New York: Penguin Press, 2016.

Hill, Logan. "What the Hell Happened to Dating?" Glamour. June 9, 2014. Accessed June 1, 2017. http://www.glamour.com/story/date-night-what- happened-to-dating.

Jafar, Afshan. "Disney's Frozen–A Lukewarm Attempt at Feminism." Gender & Society. September 5, 2014. Accessed June 1, 2017. https://genderso- ciety.wordpress.com/2014/09/05/disneys-frozen-a-lukewarm-attempt-at- feminism/.

Aronson, Elliot. *The Social Animal, tenth edition.* New York: Worth Publishers, 2008, 181–182.

Perel, Esther. "It's time to bring back relationship accountability." Esther Perel. January 25, 2017. Accessed June 1, 2017. http://www.estherperel.com/rela- tionship-accountability/.

Chen, Jason. "'Benching' Is the New Ghosting." Beta Male. June 9, 2016. Accessed June 1, 2017. http://nymag.com/betamale/2016/06/benching-ghosting.html.

Invisible Boyfriend. Accessed June 1, 2017. https://invisibleboyfriend.com/blog/can-we-solve-the-dating-gap.

Hancock, Jeffrey T.; Toma, Catalina; and Ellison, Nicole. "The Truth About Lying in Online Dating Profiles." *Proceedings of the SIGCHI Conference on Human Factors in Computing Systems - CHI 07*, 2007. doi:10.1145/1240624.1240697.

SciShow. YouTube. July 1, 2012. Accessed June 1, 2017. https://www.youtube.com/watch?v=MX3Hu8loXTE.

Nakayama, Hiroko. "Changes in the affect of infants before and after episodes of crying." *Infant Behavior and Development* 36, no. 4 (2013): 507–12. doi:10.1016/j.infbeh.2013.04.005.

University of Massachusetts at Amherst. "UMass researcher finds most people lie in everyday conversation." News release, June 10, 2002. Eureka Alert. Accessed June 1, 2017. https://www.eurekalert.org/pub_releases/2002–06/uoma-urf061002.php.

Brizendine, Louann. *The Male Brain: A Breakthrough Understanding of How Men and Boys Think*. New York: Broadway Books, 2010, p. 62.

CHAPTER 2

James, Aaron. *Assholes: a Theory*. New York: Anchor Books, 2014, 6

"Advice Goddess | Nice Guys Are from Uranus?" Advicegoddess.com: The Official Amy Alkon Website. Accessed June 1, 2017. http://www.advicegoddess.com/columns/column18.html.

Lue, Natalie. "Defining Assclowns: Men you shouldn't want to date: Part One." Baggage Reclaim by Natalie Lue. June 4, 2009. Accessed June 1, 2017. http://www.baggagereclaim.co.uk/defining-assclowns-part-one/.

Kaufman, Scott Barry. "Do Assholes Really Finish First?" Psychology Today. October 2, 2009. Accessed June 1, 2017. https://www.psychologytoday.com/blog/beautiful-minds/200910/do-assholes-really-finish-first.

Durante, Kristina M.; Griskevicius, Vladas; Simpson, Jeffry A.; Cantú, Stephanie M.; and Li, Norman P. "Ovulation leads women to perceive sexy cads as good dads." *Journal of Personality and Social Psychology* 103, no. 2 (2012): 292–305. doi:10.1037/a0028498.

Birnbaum, Gurit E.; Ein-Dor, Tsachi; Reis, Harry T.; and Segal, Noam. "Why Do Men Prefer Nice Women? Gender Typicality Mediates the Effect of Responsiveness on Perceived Attractiveness in Initial Acquaintanceships."

Personality and Social Psychology Bulletin 40, no. 10 (2014): 1341–353. doi:10.1177/0146167214543879.

Gilbert, Katie and Meyers, Seth. "Why Women Love & Lust After Unavailable Men: Traumatic Love." Psychology Today. June 28, 2012. Accessed June 1, 2017. https://www.psychologytoday.com/blog/insight-is-2020/201206/why-women-love-lust-after-unavailable-men-traumatic-love.

Katz, Evan Marc. "Do You Keep Falling for Jerks?" May 31, 2013. Accessed June 1, 2017. http://www.evanmarckatz.com/blog/dating-tips-advice/do-you-keep-falling-for-jerks/.

Morrison, Mike and Roese, Neal J. "Regrets of the Typical American." *Social Psychological and Personality Science* 2, no. 6 (2011): 576–83. doi:10.1177/19485506 11401756.

Webb, Jonice. "When the Narcissist Becomes Dangerous." Psych Central.com. Accessed June 1, 2017. https://blogs.psychcentral.com/childhood-neglect /2014/12/when-the-narcissist-becomes-dangerous/.

Campbell, W. Keith. *When You Love a Man Who Loves Himself.* Naperville, IL: Sourcebooks, Inc., 2005, p. 149.

Eastwick, Paul W.; Harden, K. Paige; Shukusky, Jennifer A.; Morgan, Taylor Anne; and Joel, Samantha. "Consistency and inconsistency among romantic partners over time." *Journal of Personality and Social Psychology* 112, no. 6 (2017): 838–59. doi:10.1037/pspi0000087.

Editors, CNT. "The Friendliest and Unfriendliest Cities in the U.S." Condé Nast Traveler. August 11, 2016. Accessed June 1, 2017. http://www.cntraveler. com/galleries/2015-08-11/the-2015-friendliest-and-unfriendliest-cities-in-the-us.

Freud, Sigmund. *Beyond the Pleasure Principle.* New York: W. W. Norton & Company, 1920, 18

CHAPTER 3

"Key Statistics from the National Survey of Family Growth - S Listing." Centers for Disease Control and Prevention. August 12, 2015. Accessed June 1, 2017. https://www.cdc.gov/nchs/nsfg/key_statistics/s.htm#sexualactivity.

Chandra, Anjani; Copen, Casey E.; and Mosher, William D. "Sexual Behavior, Sexual Attraction, and Sexual Identity in the United States: Data from the 2006–2010 National Survey of Family Growth." *International Handbook on the Demography of Sexuality International Handbooks of Population*, 2013, 17–18. doi:10.1007/978-94-007-5512-3_4.

Smith, C. Veronica and Shaffer, Matthew J. "Gone But Not Forgotten: Virginity Loss and Current Sexual Satisfaction." *Journal of Sex & Marital Therapy* 39, no. 2 (2013): 96–111. doi:10.1080/0092623x.2012.675023.

Boundless. "Freud's Psychosexual Theory of Development - Boundless Open Textbook." Boundless. September 20, 2016. Accessed June 1, 2017. https://www.boundless.com/psychology/textbooks/boundless-psychology-text-book/human-development-14/theories-of-human-development-70/freud-s-psychosexual-theory-of-development-267-12802/.

Raby, K. Lee; Roisman, Glenn I.; Fraley, R. Chris; and Simpson, Jeffry A. "The Enduring Predictive Significance of Early Maternal Sensitivity: Social and Academic Competence Through Age 32 Years." *Child Development* 86, no. 3 (2014): 695–708. doi:10.1111/cdev.12325.

Vrangalova, Zhana. TEDxTalks. "Is Casual Sex Bad for You?" TEDxCollegeof-William&Mary. June 30, 2015. Accessed June 1, 2017. https://www.youtube.com/watch?v=Soe7yjlFEJ8.

Garcia, Justin R.; Reiber, Chris; Massey, Sean G.; and Merriwether, Ann M. "Sexual hook-up culture." *Monitor on Psychology* 44, no. 2 (February 2013): 60. doi:10.1037/e505012013-009.

Rhodan, Maya. "No Satisfaction: Women Are Less Likely to Orgasm During Casual Sex." Time. November 11, 2013. Accessed June 1, 2017. http://healthland.time.com/2013/11/11/no-satisfaction-woman-are-less-likely-to-orgasm-during-casual-sex/.

Clark, Russell and Hatfield, Elaine. "Gender Differences in Receptivity to Sexual Offers." *Journal of Psychology & Human Sexuality* 2, no. 1 (1989): 39–55. doi:10.1300/j056v02n01_04.

Salamon, Maureen. "11 Interesting Effects of Oxytocin." LiveScience. December 3, 2010. Accessed June 1, 2017. http://www.livescience.com/35219-11-effects-of-oxytocin.html.

Scheele, D.; Wille, A.; Kendrick, K.M.; Stoffel-Wagner, B.; Becker, B.; Gunturkun, O.; Maier, W.; and Hurlemann, R. "Oxytocin enhances brain reward system responses in men viewing the face of their female partner." *Proceedings of the National Academy of Sciences* 110, no. 50 (2013): 20308–0313. doi:10.1073/pnas.1314190110.

Brizendine, Louann. *The Male Brain: A Breakthrough Understanding of How Men and Boys Think*. New York: Broadway Books, 2010, p. 60–61.

Superdrug.com. "What's Your Number?" What's Your Number? | Superdrug™. Accessed June 1, 2017. https://onlinedoctor.superdrug.com/whats-your-number/.

Fisher, Terri D. "Gender Roles and Pressure to be Truthful: The Bogus Pipeline Modifies Gender Differences in Sexual but Not Non-sexual Behavior." *Sex Roles* 68, no. 7–8 (2013): 401–14. doi:10.1007/s11199-013-0266-3.

Stockton, Chrissy. "I Asked A 'Nice Guy' How Many Guys A Girl Can Sleep With Before She's A Slut." Thought Catalog. December 21, 2014. Accessed June 1, 2017. http://thoughtcatalog.com/christine-stockton/2014/12/i-asked-a-nice-guy-how-many-guys-a-girl-can-sleep-with-before-shes-a-slut/.

Valenti, Jessica. *He's a Stud, She's a Slut.* Berkeley, CA: Seal Press, 2009, 15.

"Key Statistics from the National Survey of Family Growth - N Listing." Centers for Disease Control and Prevention. July 28, 2015. Accessed June 1, 2017. https://www.cdc.gov/nchs/nsfg/key_statistics/n.htm#numberlifetime.

OkCupid. "A Digital Decade: Sex – How sexual opinions and behavior have changed from 2005 to 2015." The OkCupid Blog. February 5, 2016. Accessed June 1, 2017. https://theblog.okcupid.com/a-digital-decade-sex-c95e6fb6296b.

Twenge, Jean M.; Sherman, Ryne A.; and Wells, Brooke E. "Sexual Inactivity During Young Adulthood Is More Common Among U.S. Millennials and iGen: Age, Period, and Cohort Effects on Having No Sexual Partners After Age 18." *Archives of Sexual Behavior* 46, no. 2 (2016): 433–40. doi:10.1007/s10508-016-0798-z.

Rapaport, Lisa. "Americans are having less sex these days." Reuters. March 15, 2017. Accessed June 1, 2017. http://www.reuters.com/article/us-health-sex-u-s-decline-idUSKBN16M1YO.

Muise, Amy; Schimmack, Ulrich; and Impett, Emily A. "Sexual Frequency Predicts Greater Well-Being, But More is Not Always Better." *Social Psychological and Personality Science* 7, no. 4 (2016): 295–302. doi:10.1177/1948550615616462.

Loewenstein, George; Krishnamurti, Tamar; Kopsic, Jessica; and McDonald, Daniel. "Does Increased Sexual Frequency Enhance Happiness?" *Journal of Economic Behavior & Organization* 116 (2015): 206–18. doi:10.1016/j.jebo.2015.04.021.

Blanchflower, David and Oswald, Andrew. "Money, Sex, and Happiness: An Empirical Study." 2004. doi:10.3386/w10499.

Stephens-Davidowitz, Seth. "Opinion | Searching for Sex." The New York Times. January 24, 2015. Accessed June 1, 2017. https://www.nytimes.com/2015/01/25/opinion/sunday/seth-stephens-davidowitz-searching-for-sex.html.

Parker-Pope, Tara. "When Sex Leaves the Marriage." The New York Times. June 3, 2009. Accessed June 1, 2017. https://well.blogs.nytimes.com/2009/06/03/when-sex-leaves-the-marriage/.

Bergner, Daniel. "Unexcited? There May Be a Pill for That." The New York Times. May 22, 2013. Accessed June 1, 2017. http://www.nytimes.com/2013/05/26/magazine/unexcited-there-may-be-a-pill-for-that.html.

Jio, Sarah. "8 Reasons He Doesn't Want to Have Sex." Woman's Day. September 24, 2009. Accessed June 1, 2017. http://www.womansday.com/relationships/sex-tips/a967/8-reasons-he-doesnt-want-to-have-sex-91131/.

Ryan, Christopher. "Don't Ask the Sexperts (#1)." Psychology Today. March 8, 2008. Accessed June 1, 2017. https://www.psychologytoday.com/blog/sex-dawn/200803/dont-ask-the-sexperts-1.

"Sex Question Friday: Why Can't I Maintain Sexual Interest In One Person?" Sex And Psychology. December 26, 2014. Accessed June 1, 2017. http://www.lehmiller.com/blog/2014/12/19/sex-question-friday-why-cant-i-maintain-sexual-interest-in-one-person.

Bell, Vaughan. "The unsexy truth about dopamine." The Observer. February 2, 2013. Accessed June 1, 2017. https://www.theguardian.com/science/2013/feb/03/dopamine-the-unsexy-truth.

Morton, Heather and Gorzalka, Boris B. "Role of Partner Novelty in Sexual Functioning: A Review." *Journal of Sex & Marital Therapy* 41, no. 6 (2014): 593–609. doi:10.1080/0092623x.2014.958788.

"Is Long-Term Love More Than a Rare Phenomenon? If So, What Are Its Correlates?" Reuniting. Accessed June 1, 2017. https://www.reuniting.info/science/sex_in_the_brain.

Geary, David C., Vigil, Jacob, and Byrd-Craven, Jennifer. "Evolution of human mate choice." *The Journal of Sex Research* 41 (2004): 27–42.

Wilson, Gary. "The great porn experiment." TEDxTalks. TEDxGlasgow. May 16, 2012. Accessed June 1, 2017. https://www.youtube.com/watch?v=wSF82AwSDiU.

Rothbart, Davy. "He's Just Not That Into Anyone." NYMag.com. January 30, 2011. Accessed June 1, 2017. http://nymag.com/news/features/70976/index1.html.

Grubbs, Joshua B.; Stauner, Nicholas; Exline, Julie J.; Pargament, Kenneth I.; and Lindberg, Matthew J. "Perceived addiction to Internet pornography and psychological distress: Examining relationships concurrently and over time." *Psychology of Addictive Behaviors* 29, no. 4 (2015): 1056–067. doi:10.1037/adb0000114.

Emery, Lea Rose. "This Is How Many Women Watch Porn Every Week." Bustle. October 21, 2015. Accessed June 1, 2017. https://www.bustle.com/articles/118394-this-is-how-many-women-watch-porn-every-week.

Hot Girls Wanted: Turned On. Directed by Jill Bauer, Ronna Gradus, and Rashida Jones. 2017. https://www.netflix.com/title/80115676.

Ogas, Ogi and Gaddam, Sai. *A Billion Wicked Thoughts: What the Internet Tells Us About Sexual Relationships.* New York: Plume, 2012,174–178.

"Catalyst Home." Catalyst: The Science of Dating: "How to Catch a Mate" - ABC TV Science. March 3, 2007. Accessed June 1, 2017. http://www.abc.net.au/catalyst/stories/s1878168.htm.

Ingraham, Christopher. "Sex toy injuries surged after 'Fifty Shades of Grey' was published." The Washington Post. February 10, 2015. Accessed June 1, 2017. https://www.washingtonpost.com/news/wonk/wp/2015/02/10/sex-toy-injuries-surged-after-fifty-shades-of-grey-was-published/.

"National Electronic Injury Surveillance System (NEISS)." CPSC.gov. March 23, 2017. Accessed June 1, 2017. https://www.cpsc.gov/Research—Statistics/NEISS-Injury-Data/.

"Adult Stores in the US Industry Market Research Report Now Available from IBISWorld." PRWeb. December 24, 2013. Accessed June 1, 2017. http://www.prweb.com/releases/2013/12/prweb11447526.htm.

Mollen, Jenny. "*Fifty Shades of Grey* Changed My Sex Life." Cosmopolitan. May 26, 2014. Accessed June 1, 2017. http://www.cosmopolitan.com/sex-love/advice/a6936/fifty-shades-of-grey-confession/.

Joyal, Christian C.; Cossette, Amélie; and Lapierre, Vanessa. "What Exactly Is an Unusual Sexual Fantasy?" *The Journal of Sexual Medicine* 12, no. 2 (2015): 328–40. doi:10.1111/jsm.12734.

CHAPTER 4

Jagel, Katie. "Heartbreak: More common in America?" YouGov: What the world thinks. December 5, 2013. Accessed June 1, 2017. https://today.yougov.com/news/2013/12/05/heart-break/.

"Average woman will kiss 15 men and be heartbroken twice before meeting 'The One', study reveals." *The Telegraph*. January 1, 2014. Accessed June 1, 2017. http://www.telegraph.co.uk/news/picturegalleries/howaboutthat/10545810

/Average-woman-will-kiss-15-men-and-be-heartbroken-twice-before-meeting-The-One-study-reveals.html.

"Is Broken Heart Syndrome Real?" April 18, 2016. American Heart Association. Accessed June 1, 2017. http://www.heart.org/HEARTORG/Conditions/More/Cardiomyopathy/Is-Broken-Heart-Syndrome-Real_UCM_448547_Article.jsp#.WS_S9xMrLfZ.

Fisher, H. E.; Brown, Lucy L.; Aron, Arthur; Strong, Greg; and Mashek, Debra. "Reward, Addiction, and Emotion Regulation Systems Associated With Rejection in Love." *Journal of Neurophysiology* Vol. 104, no. 1 (2010): 51–60. doi:10.1152/jn.00784.2009.

Kross, Ethan; Berman, Marc G.; Mischel, Walter; Smith, Edward E.; and Wager, Tor D. "Social rejection shares somatosensory representations with physical pain." *Proceedings of the National Academy of Sciences* Vol. 108, no. 15 (2011): 6270–275. doi:10.1073/pnas.1102693108.

Rhoades, Galena K.; Kamp Dush, Claire M.; Atkins, David C.; Stanley, Scott M.; and Markman, Howard J. "Breaking up is hard to do: The impact of unmarried relationship dissolution on mental health and life satisfaction." *Journal of Family Psychology* Vol. 25, no. 3 (2011): 366–74. doi:10.1037/a0023627.

Gilbert, Steven P. and Sifers, Sarah K. "Bouncing Back from a Breakup: Attachment, Time Perspective, Mental Health, and Romantic Loss." *Journal of College Student Psychotherapy* 25, no. 4 (2011): 295–310. doi:10.1080/87568225.2011.605693.

Parker-Pope, Tara. "Go Easy on Yourself, a New Wave of Research Urges." The New York Times. February 28, 2011. Accessed June 1, 2017. https://well.blogs.nytimes.com/2011/02/28/go-easy-on-yourself-a-new-wave-of-research-urges/.

Kipp, Mastin. "Why It's Important To Love Yourself." Daily Love with Mastin Kipp. August 23, 2011. Accessed June 1, 2017. http://thedailylove.com/why-its-important-to-love-yourself/.

Kraft, Tara L. and Pressman, Sarah D. "Grin and Bear It." *Psychological Science* 23, no. 11 (2012): 1372–378. doi:10.1177/0956797612445312.

Joelving, Frederik. "Why the #$%! Do We Swear? For Pain Relief." *Scientific American*. July 12, 2009. Accessed June 1, 2017. https://www.scientificamerican.com/article/why-do-we-swear/.

Bartlett, Tom. "The Importance of Hating Your Ex." *The Chronicle of Higher Education*. May 11, 2010. Accessed June 1, 2017. http://chronicle.com/blogs/percolator/the-importance-of-hating-your-ex/23900.

"The Science Behind Why Naming Our Feelings Makes Us Happier." 'Ekahi Ornish Lifestyle Medicine. Accessed June 1, 2017. https://www.ekahiornish.com/ohana/love-support/science-behind-naming-feelings-makes-us-happier/.

Esfahani Smith, Emily. "What Does 'Closure' Even Mean, Anyway?" Science of Us. February 16, 2017. Accessed June 1, 2017. http://nymag.com/scienceofus/2017/02/how-to-get-closure-after-a-breakup.html.

Doyle, Hillary H.; Eidson, Lori N.; Sinkiewicz, David M.; and Murphy, Anne Z. "Sex Differences in Microglia Activity within the Periaqueductal Gray of the Rat: A Potential Mechanism Driving the Dimorphic Effects of Morphine." *The Journal of Neuroscience* 37, no. 12 (2017): 3202–214. doi:10.1523/jneurosci.2906–16.2017.

Morris, Craig Eric; Reiber, Chris; and Roman, Emily. "Quantitative Sex Differences in Response to the Dissolution of a Romantic Relationship." *Evolutionary Behavioral Sciences* 9, no. 4 (2015): 270–82. doi:10.1037/ebs0000054.

Greenberg, Melanie. "The Neuroscience of Relationship Breakups." Psychology Today. April 17, 2011. Accessed June 1, 2017. https://www.psychologytoday.com/blog/the-mindful-self-express/201104/the-neuroscience-relationship-breakups.

"Males Believe Discussing Problems Is a Waste of Time, MU study shows." MU News Bureau. August 22, 2011. Accessed June 1, 2017. http://munews.missouri.edu/news-releases/2011/0822-males-believe-discussing-problems-is-a-waste-of-time-mu-study-shows/.

"Suicide Statistics." American Foundation for Suicide Prevention. 2015. Accessed June 1, 2017. https://www.afsp.org/understanding-suicide/facts-and-figures.

Farrelly, Daniel; Owens, Rebecca; Elliott, Hannah R.; Walden, Hannah R.; and Wetherell, Mark A. (2015). "The effects of being in a 'new relationship' on levels of testosterone in men." Evolutionary Psychology, 13, 250–261.

Orenstein, Beth W. "Testosterone: A Hormone That Works Differently in Men and Women." EverydayHealth.com. October 8, 2015. Accessed June 1, 2017. http://www.everydayhealth.com/low-testosterone-pictures/dueling-testosterone-hormones-that-works-differently-in-men-and-women.aspx#08.

Brumbaugh, Claudia C. and Fraley, R. Chris. "Too fast, too soon? An empirical investigation into rebound relationships." *Journal of Social and Personal Relationships* 32, no. 1 (2015): 99–118. doi:10.1177/0265407514525086.

Spielmann, Stephanie S.; MacDonald, Geoff; and Wilson, Anne E. "On the Rebound: Focusing on Someone New Helps Anxiously Attached Individuals Let Go of Ex-Partners." *Personality and Social Psychology Bulletin* 35, no. 10 (2009): 1382–394. doi:10.1177/0146167209341580.

Barber, Lindsay L. and Cooper, M. Lynne. "Rebound Sex: Sexual Motives and Behaviors Following a Relationship Breakup." *Archives of Sexual Behavior* 43, no. 2 (2013): 251–65. doi:10.1007/s10508-013-0200-3.

Halpern-Meekin, Sarah; Manning, Wendy D.; Giordano, Peggy C.; and Longmore, Monica A. "Relationship Churning in Emerging Adulthood: On/Off Relationships and Sex with an Ex." *Journal of Adolescent Research* 28, no. 2 (2013): 166–188. doi:10.1177/0743558412464524.

Dreher, Christopher. "The myth of closure." Boston.com. September 4, 2011. Accessed June 1, 2017. http://archive.boston.com/lifestyle/health/articles/2011/09/04/the_myth_of_closure/.

CHAPTER 5

Halvorson, Heidi Grant. "How to Walk Away." The Atlantic. May 14, 2013. Accessed June 1, 2017. https://www.theatlantic.com/health/archive/2013/05/how-to-walk-away/275833/.

Rego, Sara; Arantes, Joana; and Magalhães, Paula. "Is there a Sunk Cost Effect in Committed Relationships?" *Current Psychology*, 2016. doi:10.1007/s12144-016-9529-9.

Lee, Spike W.S. and Schwarz, Norbert. "Framing love: When it hurts to think we were made for each other." *Journal of Experimental Social Psychology* Vol. 54 (2014): 61–67. doi:10.1016/j.jesp.2014.04.007.

Mandell, Andrea. "Is 'La La Land's ending happy or sad? We're still debating." USA Today. February 21, 2017. Accessed June 1, 2017. https://www.usatoday.com/story/life/movies/2017/02/21/spoilers-la-la-land-dream-sequence-ending-meaning/98164730/.

Harrell, Eben. "Are Romantic Movies Bad For You?" Time. December 23, 2008. Accessed June 1, 2017. http://content.time.com/time/health/article/0,8599,1868389,00.html.

Grizzard, Matthew; Shaw, Allison Z.; Dolan, Emily A.; Anderson, Kenton B.; Hahn, Lindsay; and Prabhu, Sujay. "Does Repeated Exposure to Popular Media Strengthen Moral Intuitions?: Exploratory Evidence Regarding Consistent and Conflicted Moral Content." *Media Psychology*, 2016, 1–27. doi:10.1080/15213269.2016.1227266.

Botton, Alain De. "Opinion | Why You Will Marry the Wrong Person." *The New York Times*. May 28, 2016. Accessed June 1, 2017. https://www.nytimes.

com/2016/05/29/opinion/sunday/why-you-will-marry-the-wrong-person. html?_r=0.

"The Odds of Finding Life and Love." It's Okay To Be Smart. February 11, 2013. Accessed June 1, 2017. https://www.youtube.com/watch?time_continue=1&v=TekbxvnvYb8.

Munroe, Randall. "Soul Mates." What If? Accessed June 1, 2017. https://what-if. xkcd.com/9/.

Stein, Joel. "Millennials: The Me Me Me Generation." *Time.* May 20, 2013. Accessed June 1, 2017. http://time.com/247/millennials-the-me-me-me-generation/.

Wang, Helen H. "The Real Reason Chinese Millennials Are Super Consumers." Forbes. March 27, 2017. Accessed June 1, 2017. https://www.forbes.com/ sites/helenwang/2017/03/27/the-real-reason-chinese-millennials-are-super-consumers/#3403f2b64053.

CHAPTER 6

Schlessinger, Laura. "When to Give an Ultimatum." Dr. Laura Blog. Accessed June 1, 2017. https://www.drlaura.com/b/When-to-Give-an-Ultimatum /533790317891224371.html.

Scotti, Dan. "Why The Person Who Cares Less Always Has The Power In A Relationship." Elite Daily. June 11, 2015. Accessed June 1, 2017. http://elite-daily.com/dating/person-cares-less-always-power-relationship/1063660/.

Buckley, Rhonda R. "Principle of Least Interest." *The Wiley Blackwell Encyclopedia of Family Studies*, 2016, 1–2. doi:10.1002/9781119085621.wbefs288.

CHAPTER 7

"Marriage and Divorce." Centers for Disease Control and Prevention. March 17, 2017. Accessed June 1, 2017. https://www.cdc.gov/nchs/fastats/marriage-divorce.htm.

Wolfinger, Nicholas H. "Revisiting the Relationship between Age at Marriage and Divorce." Nicholas H. Wolfinger. Accessed June 1, 2017. http://www. nicholaswolfinger.com/blog/2015/04/29/revisiting-the-relationship-be-tween-age-at-marriage-and-divorce/.

Olson, Randal S. "144 years of marriage and divorce in 1 chart." Randal S. Olson. June 15, 2015. Accessed June 1, 2017. http://www.randalolson. com/2015/06/15/144-years-of-marriage-and-divorce-in-1-chart/.

Leonhardt, David and Quealy, Kevin. "How Your Hometown Affects Your Chances of Marriage." *The New York Times.* May 15, 2015. Accessed June 1, 2017.

https://www.nytimes.com/interactive/2015/05/15/upshot/the-places-that-discourage-marriage-most.html.

Downey, Allen. " Millennials are still not getting married." Probably Overthinking It. October 14, 2016. Accessed June 1, 2017. http://allendowney.blogspot.ca/2016/10/millennials-are-still-not-getting.html.

Wang, Wendy and Parker, Kim. "Record Share of Americans Have Never Married." Pew Research Center's Social & Demographic Trends Project. September 24, 2014. Accessed June 1, 2017. http://www.pewsocialtrends.org/2014/09/24/record-share-of-americans-have-never-married/.

"The 1960s-70s American Feminist Movement: Breaking Down Barriers for Women." Tavaana. Accessed June 1, 2017. https://tavaana.org/en/content/1960s-70s-american-feminist-movement-breaking-down-barriers-women.

Goldin, Claudia and Katz, Lawrence F. 2002. "The power of the pill: Oral contraceptives and women's career and marriage decisions." *Journal of Political Economy* 110(4): 730–770. doi:10.1086/340778.

Shamsian, Jacob. "The common statistic that 'half of marriages end in divorce' is bogus." INSIDER. February 9, 2017. Accessed June 1, 2017. http://www.thisisinsider.com/what-is-the-divorce-rate-2017-2.

Francis, David R. "Why Do Women Outnumber Men in College?" The National Bureau of Economic Research. Accessed June 1, 2017. http://www.nber.org/digest/jan07/w12139.html.

"World Marriage Data 2008." United Nations, Department of Economic and Social Affairs, Population Division. 2008.

Cohen, Philip N. "Marriage is declining globally: Can you say that?" Family Inequality. June 12, 2013. Accessed June 1, 2017. https://familyinequality.wordpress.com/2013/06/12/marriage-is-declining/.

"Singles in America: Match.com Releases Its Fourth Annual Comprehensive Study on Singles." Match.com MediaRoom. February 5, 2014. Accessed June 1, 2017. http://match.mediaroom.com/2014-02-05-Singles-in-America-Match-com-Releases-Its-Fourth-Annual-Comprehensive-Study-on-Singles.

Mills, Michael. "Why Don't Women Ask Men Out on First Dates?" Psychology Today. April 30, 2011. Accessed June 1, 2017. https://www.psychologytoday.com/blog/the-how-and-why-sex-differences/201104/why-dont-women-ask-men-out-first-dates.

Mark, Joshua J. "Love, Sex, and Marriage in Ancient Mesopotamia." Ancient History Encyclopedia. May 16, 2014. Accessed June 1, 2017. http://www.ancient.eu/article/688/.

Bertman, Stephen. *Handbook to Life in Ancient Mesopotamia*. New York: Facts on File, 2002, 287.

Gadoua, Susan Pease and Larson, Vicki. *The New "I Do": Reshaping Marriage for Skeptics, Realists, and Rebels*. Berkeley, CA: Seal Press, 2014, p. 22.

"How marriage has changed over centuries." The Week. June 1, 2012. Accessed June 1, 2017. http://theweek.com/articles/475141/how-marriage-changed-over-centuries.

Halper, Katie. "Sex at Dawn: 9 Interesting Things We've Learned About Sex From Studying Our Ancient Ancestors." Alternet. March 4, 2013. Accessed June 1, 2017. http://www.alternet.org/sex-dawn-9-interesting-things-weve-learned-about-sex-studying-our-ancient-ancestors.

Rogers, Thomas. ""Sex at Dawn": Why monogamy goes against our nature." Salon. June 27, 2010. Accessed June 1, 2017. http://www.salon.com/2010/06/27/sex_at_dawn_interview/.

Haupert, M. L.; Gesselman, Amanda N.; Moors, Amy C.; Fisher, Helen E.; and Garcia, Justin R. "Prevalence of Experiences With Consensual Nonmonogamous Relationships: Findings From Two National Samples of Single Americans." *Journal of Sex & Marital Therapy*, 2016, 1–17. doi:10.1080/0092 623x.2016.1178675.

Baer, Drake. "Maybe Monogamy Isn't the Only Way to Love." Science of Us. March 6, 2017. Accessed June 1, 2017. http://nymag.com/scienceofus/2017/03/science-of-polyamory-open-relationships-and-nonmonogamy.html.

Grinberg, Emanuella. "Polyamorous community welcomes OkCupid feature for open relationships." CNN. January 9, 2016. Accessed June 1, 2017. http://www.cnn.com/2016/01/08/living/okcupid-polyamorous-open-relationships-feat/.

Ley, David J. "Why Is Monogamy Idealized When Most People Aren't Monogamous?" Alternet. June 17, 2012. Accessed June 1, 2017. http://www.alternet.org/story/155904/why_is_monogamy_idealized_when_most_people_aren't_monogamous.

Henrich, Joseph; Boyd, Robert; and Richerson, Peter J. "The puzzle of monogamous marriage." Philosophical Transactions of the Royal Society B. January 23, 2012. Accessed June 1, 2017. http://rstb.royalsocietypublishing.org/content/367/1589/657.

Allen, Samantha. "Polygamy Is More Popular Than Ever." The Daily Beast. June 2, 2015. Accessed June 1, 2017. http://www.thedailybeast.com/articles/2015/06/02/polygamy-is-more-popular-than-ever.

Nelson, Tammy. "Are We Meant To Be Monogamous? Why People Cheat, And The Appeal Of Open Relationships." The Independent. March 10, 2015. Accessed June 1, 2017. http://www.independent.co.uk/life-style/love-sex/are-we-meant-to-be-monogamous-why-people-cheat-open-relationships-and-life-after-an-affair-10097811.html.

Luscombe, Belinda. "What Drove Man to Monogamy: It Wasn't Love." *Time*. July 30, 2013. Accessed June 1, 2017. http://healthland.time.com/2013/07/30/the-reason-for-monogamy-researchers-disagree/?awc=5160_1496313545_7b9a7fea2154dd011dd390db9e411034.

Mayyasi, Alex. "At What Age Do People Get Married Around the World?" Priceonomics. May 16, 2016. Accessed June 1, 2017. https://priceonomics.com/at-what-age-do-people-get-married-around-the-world/.

Aleccia, Jonel. "'The new normal': Cohabitation on the rise, study finds." NBCNews.com. April 4, 2013. Accessed June 1, 2017. http://www.nbcnews.com/health/new-normal-cohabitation-rise-study-finds-1C9208429.

Rettner, Rachael. "Marriage, Cohabitation Provide Similar Health Benefit." LiveScience. January 19, 2012. Accessed June 1, 2017. http://www.livescience.com/18026-marriage-cohabitation-benefits.html.

CHAPTER 8

Wolchover, Natalie. "Why Everyone Believes in Magic (Even You)." LiveScience. April 12, 2012. Accessed June 1, 2017. http://www.livescience.com/19665-belief-magic.html.

Schoener, Gustav-Adolf. "Astrology: Between Religion and the Empirical." Accessed June 1, 2017. http://www.esoteric.msu.edu/VolumeIV/astrology.htm.

Lewis, James R. *The Astrology Book: The Encyclopedia of Heavenly Influences*. Detroit, MI: Visible Ink, 2003, p. 318.

"Astrology: Is it scientific?" Accessed June 1, 2017. http://undsci.berkeley.edu/article/astrology_checklist.

"Psychic Services: Market Research Report." IBISWorld. December 2016. Accessed June 1, 2017. https://www.ibisworld.com/industry/psychic-services.html.

"America's Changing Religious Landscape." Pew Research Center's Religion & Public Life Project. May 12, 2015. Accessed June 1, 2017. http://www.pewforum.org/2015/05/12/americas-changing-religious-landscape/.

Kiersz, Andy. "Religion in America is on the decline." Business Insider. June 18, 2015. Accessed June 1, 2017. http://www.businessinsider.com/organized-religion-is-on-the-decline-in-america-2015-6.

Botero, Carlos A.; Gardner, Beth; Kirby, Kathryn R.; Bulbulia, Joseph; Gavin, Michael C.; and Gray, Russell D. "The ecology of religious beliefs." *Proceedings of the National Academy of Sciences of the United States of America,* 111 (47), 16784–16789, 10.1073/pnas.1408701111

Grad, Shelby, and Colker, David. "Nancy Reagan turned to astrology in White House to protect her husband." Los Angeles Times. March 6, 2016. Accessed June 1, 2017. http://www.latimes.com/local/lanow/la-me-ln-nancy-reagan-astrology-20160306-story.html.

Vyse, Stuart A. *Believing in Magic: The Psychology of Superstition.* Oxford: Oxford University Press, 2000, p. 144.

"Science and Engineering Indicators 2014." S&E Indicators 2014 - Chapter 7. Science and Technology: Public Attitudes and Understanding - Highlights - US National Science Foundation (NSF). Accessed June 1, 2017. https://www.nsf.gov/statistics/seind14/index.cfm/chapter-7/c7h.htm.

Crowson, T. W.; Rich, E. C.; and Harris, I. B. "A comparison of locus of control between men and women in an internal medicine residency." *Academic Medicine* 61, no. 10 (1986): 840–1. doi:10.1097/00001888-198610000-00011.

Khorshidifar, Mahbobeh, and Abedi, Ali. "An empirical study on the impact of stress on the relationship between locus of control and job satisfaction and job performance." *Management Science Letters* 1, no. 4 (2011): 511–16. doi:10.5267/j.msl.2011.05.007.

Sherman, Adrian C.; Higgs, Graham E.; and Williams, Robert L. "Gender differences in the locus of control construct." *Psychology & Health* Vol. 12, no. 2 (1997): 239–48. doi:10.1080/08870449708407402.

Brizendine, Louann. *The Female Brain.* London: Bantam, 2007, p. 120–123.

CHAPTER 9

Blackwood, Emily. "Grown-Ass Women Don't Let Guys Ruin Friendships." YourTango. August 9, 2016. Accessed June 1, 2017. http://www.yourtango.com/2016293629/grown-women-dont-let-men-ruin-friendships.

Day, Heather Thompson. "To The Girl Who Slept With My Boyfriend." Thought Catalog. March 30, 2017. Accessed June 1, 2017. http://thoughtcatalog.com/heather-thompson-day/2017/03/to-the-girl-who-slept-with-my-boyfriend/.

Stockley, P. and Campbell, A. "Female competition and aggression: interdisciplinary perspectives." *Philosophical Transactions of the Royal Society B: Biological Sciences* 368, no. 1631 (2013): 20130073. doi:10.1098/rstb.2013.0073.

Fisher, Maryanne, and Cox, Anthony. "Four strategies used during intrasexual competition for mates." *Personal Relationships* Vol. 18, no. 1 (2010): 20–38. doi:10.1111/j.1475–6811.2010.01307.x.

Engelhaupt, Erika. "Maybe mean girls' mental games have a purpose." Science News. October 31, 2013. Accessed June 1, 2017. https://www.sciencenews.org/blog/gory-details/maybe-mean-girls-mental-games-have-purpose.

"New Demos study reveals scale of social media misogyny." Demos. May 26, 2016. Accessed June 1, 2017. https://www.demos.co.uk/press-release/staggering-scale-of-social-media-misogyny-mapped-in-new-demos-study/.

Schmitt, David P. "Patterns and Universals of Mate Poaching Across 53 Nations: The Effects of Sex, Culture, and Personality on Romantically Attracting Another Person's Partner." *Journal of Personality and Social Psychology* Vol. 86, no. 4 (2004): 560–84. doi:10.1037/0022–3514.86.4.560.

Vaillancourt, Tracy and Sharma, Aanchal. "Intolerance of sexy peers: intrasexual competition among women." *Aggressive Behavior* 37, no. 6 (2011): 569–77. doi:10.1002/ab.20413.

Khazan, Olga. "The Evolution of Bitchiness." The Atlantic. November 20, 2013. Accessed June 1, 2017. https://www.theatlantic.com/health/archive/2013/11/the-evolution-of-bitchiness/281657/.

Buss, David. "Female Sexual Psychology." World Question Center. Accessed June 1, 2017. https://www.edge.org/q2008/q08_12.html#buss.

Schmitt, David P. "Are men universally more dismissing than women? Gender differences in romantic attachment across 62 cultural regions." *Personal Relationships* Vol. 10, no. 3 (2003): 307–31. doi:10.1111/1475–6811.00052.

Birger, Jon. *Date-Onomics: How Dating Became a Lopsided Numbers Game.* New York: Workman Publishing, 2015.

Adams, Stephen. "Women like to 'poach' attached men." The Telegraph. August 14, 2009. Accessed June 1, 2017. http://www.telegraph.co.uk/news/science/science-news/6025978/Women-like-to-poach-attached-men.html.

Tierney, John. "Why Poach Another's Mate? Ask An Expert." *The New York Times.* August 27, 2009. Accessed June 1, 2017. https://tierneylab.blogs.nytimes.com/2009/08/27/why-poach-anothers-mate-ask-an-expert-or-brangelina/comment-page-4/?_r=0.

Tierney, John. "Do Single Women Seek Attached Men?" *The New York Times*. August 13, 2009. Accessed June 1, 2017. https://tierneylab.blogs.nytimes. com/2009/08/13/do-single-women-seek-attached-men/?mtrref=undefined&_r=0.

Schmitt, David P. and Buss, David M. "Human mate poaching: Tactics and temptations for infiltrating existing mateships." *Journal of Personality and Social Psychology* 80, no. 6 (2001): 894–917. doi:10.1037//0022–3514.80.6.894.

Reis, Harry T. *Encyclopedia of Human Relationships*. Los Angeles: SAGE, 2009.

Schmitt, David P. "Patterns and Universals of Mate Poaching Across 53 Nations: The Effects of Sex, Culture, and Personality on Romantically Attracting Another Person's Partner." *Journal of Personality and Social Psychology* Vol. 86, no. 4 (2004): 560–84. doi:10.1037/0022–3514.86.4.560.

Zaslow, Jeffrey. "Friendship for Guys (No Tears!)." *The Wall Street Journal*. April 7, 2010. Accessed June 1, 2017. https://www.wsj.com/articles/SB1000142405 2702304620304575166090090482912.

Taylor, Shelley E., Klein, Laura Cousino; Lewis, Brian P.; Gruenewald, Tara L.; Gurung, Regan A. R.; and Updegraff, John A. "Biobehavioral Responses to Stress in Females: Tend-and-Befriend, Not Fight-or-Flight." *Psychological Review* Vol. 107, no. 3 (2000): 411–29. doi:10.1037//0033-295x.107.3.411.

Waxler-Morrison, Nancy; Hislop, T. Gregory; Mears, Bronwen; and Kan, Lisa. "Effects of social relationships on survival for women with breast cancer: A prospective study." *Social Science & Medicine* Vol. 33, no. 2 (1991): 177–83. doi:10.1016/0277–9536(91)90178-f.

CHAPTER 10

Harris, Christine. "The Evolution of Jealousy." *American Scientist* Vol. 92, no. 1 (2004): 62. doi:10.1511/2004.45.919.

"Over 75% of people lie on social media." Naked Security. April 7, 2016. Accessed June 1, 2017. https://nakedsecurity.sophos.com/2016/04/07/over-75-of-people-lie-on-social-media/.

Fessenden, Marissa. "Create Your Very Own False Memories by Lying on Facebook." Smithsonian.com. January 2, 2015. Accessed June 1, 2017. http://www.smithsonianmag.com/smart-news/create-your-very-own-false-memories-lying-facebook-180953796/.

"Leon Festinger's Social Comparison Theory." The Psychology Notes Headquarters. Accessed June 11, 2017. https://www.psychologynoteshq.com/leonfestinger-socialcomparisontheory/.

Emmons, Robert A. and McCullough, Michael E. "Counting blessings versus burdens: An experimental investigation of gratitude and subjective well-being in daily life." *Journal of Personality and Social Psychology* Vol. 84, no. 2 (2003): 377–89. doi:10.1037/0022–3514.84.2.377.

News, ABC. "Many Would Rather Be Anything but Obese." ABC News. May 23, 2006. Accessed June 1, 2017. http://abcnews.go.com/Technology/story?id=1990648&page=1.

Asano, Evan. "How Much Time Do People Spend on Social Media? [Infographic]." Social Media Today. January 4, 2017. Accessed June 1, 2017. http://www.socialmediatoday.com/marketing/how-much-time-do-people-spend-social-media-infographic.

Elgan, Mike. "Social media addiction is a bigger problem than you think." Computerworld. December 14, 2015. Accessed June 1, 2017. http://www.computerworld.com/article/3014439/internet/social-media-addiction-is-a-bigger-problem-than-you-think.html.

DiPietro, Louis. "Addicted to Facebook: why we keep returning | Cornell Chronicle." Cornell University. December 10, 2015. Accessed June 1, 2017. http://news.cornell.edu/stories/2015/12/addicted-facebook-why-we-keep-returning.

Kraut, Robert; Patterson, Michael; Lundmark, Vicki; Kiesler, Sara; Mukophadhyay, Tridas; and Scherlis, William. "Internet Paradox: A Social Technology That Reduces Social Involvement and Psychological Well-Being?" *American Psychologist* Vol. 53, no. 9 (1998): 1017–031. doi:10.1037//0003-066x.53.9.1017.

"More Social Connection Online Tied to Increasing Feelings of Isolation." UPMC/University of Pittsburgh Schools of the Health Sciences. March 6, 2017. Accessed June 1, 2017. http://www.upmc.com/media/NewsReleases/2017/Pages/primack-smu.aspx.

Emery, Lydia F.; Muise, Amy; Dix, Emily L.; and Le, Benjamin. "Can You Tell That I'm in a Relationship? Attachment and Relationship Visibility on Facebook." *Personality and Social Psychology Bulletin* Vol. 40, no. 11 (2014): 1466–479. doi:10.1177/0146167214549944.

Festinger, L. "A Theory of Social Comparison Processes." *Human Relations* Vol. 7, no. 2 (1954): 117–40. doi:10.1177/001872675400700202.

Lyubomirsky, Sonja. "Why are some people happier than others? The role of cognitive and motivational processes in well-being." *American Psychologist* Vol. 56, no. 3 (2001): 239–49. doi:10.1037//0003-066x.56.3.239.

"Eating Disorder Statistics." National Association of Anorexia Nervosa and Associated Disorders. Accessed June 1, 2017. http://www.anad.org/get-information/about-eating-disorders/eating-disorders-statistics/.

Lin, Liu Yi, Sidani, Jaime E.; Shensa, Ariel; Radovic, Ana; Miller, Elizabeth; Colditz, Jason B.; Hoffman, Beth L.; Giles, Leila M.; and Primack, Brian A. "Association Between Social Media Use And Depression Among U.S. Young Adults." *Depression and Anxiety* 33, no. 4 (2016): 323–31. doi:10.1002/da.22466.

Tiggemann, Marika and Miller, Jessica. "The Internet and Adolescent Girls' Weight Satisfaction and Drive for Thinness." *Sex Roles* Vol. 63, no. 1–2 (2010): 79–90. doi:10.1007/s11199-010-9789-z.

Haferkamp, Nina and Krämer, Nicole C. "Social Comparison 2.0: Examining the Effects of Online Profiles on Social-Networking Sites." *Cyberpsychology, Behavior, and Social Networking* Vol. 14, no. 5 (2011): 309–14. doi:10.1089/cyber.2010.0120.

Bargh, John A.; Chen, Mark; and Burrows, Lara. "Automaticity of social behavior: Direct effects of trait construct and stereotype activation on action." *Journal of Personality and Social Psychology* Vol. 71, no. 2 (1996): 230–44. doi:10.1037//0022–3514.71.2.230.

"The Neurology of Schadenfreude." Association for Psychological Science February 1, 2011. Accessed June 1, 2017. http://www.psychologicalscience. org/news/were-only-human/the-neurology-of-schadenfreude.html#. WTADcxMrLfZ.

"Is there such a thing as a 'schadenfreude face'?" Seriously, Science? October 22, 2014. Accessed June 1, 2017. http://blogs.discovermagazine.com/seriouslyscience/2014/10/22/face-schadenfreude-differentiation-joy-schadenfreude-electromyography/#.WNgrlRIrLfb.

Ferro, Shaunacy. "Babies Display Schadenfreude Toward People Who Are Different." Popular Science. March 12, 2013. Accessed June 1, 2017. http:// www.popsci.com/science/article/2013-03/being-mean-girl-starts-crib.

van Dijk, Wilco W. and Ouwerkerk, Jaap W. *Schadenfreude: Understanding Pleasure at the Misfortune of Others*. Cambridge: Cambridge University Press, 2016, p. 2.

Stech, Katy. "Everybody Lies on Social Media—Just Ask Bankruptcy Asset Hunters." The Wall Street Journal. December 26, 2016. Accessed June 1, 2017. https://www.wsj.com/articles/everybody-lies-on-social-mediajust-ask-bankruptcy-asset-hunters-1482767353.

Gammon, Jake. "Over a quarter of Americans have made malicious online comments." YouGov. October 20, 2014. Accessed June 1, 2017. https://today.yougov.com/news/2014/10/20/over-quarter-americans-admit-malicious-online-comm/.

Acknowledgments

A lifetime of love and gratitude to everyone who made this book possible: First and foremost, my wonderful agent, Joelle Delbourgo, and extraordinarily talented (and patient) editors at Skyhorse, Brooke Rockwell and Nicole Mele, who took a chance on this valley girl and made her dream come true. The brilliant, insightful, and patient psychologists, scientists, and masters of their trade who graciously agreed to be interviewed and shared their wisdom with me, in particular: Barry Schwartz, Louann Brizendine, Helen Fisher, Nicholas Wolfinger, David M. White, Eileen Kennedy-Moore, Mama Donna Henes, and Erin K. Smith. Mom, Dad, Sandy, and Eugene, who raised me to be able to tell my stories. My favorite ladies in the world: Pegah Shahriari, Dorothy Kim, Mary Anne Guintu, Sandra Kim, Claudia Kim, Fahiemah Al-Ali, Stephanie Zee, Donna Lee, and other friends who have provided endless love, humor, guidance, and shit-talking sessions during this process and beyond. Your friendship inspires me every day. My most-trusted confidantes, Tu Giang and Myra Cervantes, who were patient and brave enough to read and guide my early drafts, excruciating typos and all. David Standish and Connie Karambelas, who were instrumental in planting the seeds that would eventually bring this story to life. My editors at *Psychology Today* for generously allowing a lowly former intern to write about her relationship woes for a global audience. All the baristas at Starbucks and Another Cafe, you guys literally fueled everything on these pages. And, finally, my roommate, Ryan, whose love and . . . edits, candor, and patience brought this book to completion with minimal censorship. I am lucky to be able to raise two cats with you.